No-Nonsense JOB INTERVIEWS

How to Impress Prospective Employers and Ace Any Interview

Arnold G. Boldt

Certified Professional Resume Writer

Job and Career Transition Coach

CAREER PRESS

Franklin Lakes, NJ

NO-NONSENSE JOB INTERVIEWS
EDITED BY KIRSTEN DALLEY
TYPESET BY MICHAEL FITZGIBBON
Cover design by DesignConcepts
Printed in the U.S.A. by Book-mart Press

To order this title, please call toll-free 1-800-CAREER-1 (NJ and Canada: 201-848-0310) to order using VISA or MasterCard, or for further information on books from Career Press.

The Career Press, Inc., 3 Tice Road, PO Box 687,
Franklin Lakes, NJ 07417
www.careerpress.com

Library of Congress Cataloging-in-Publication Data

Information Available Upon Request

Contents

Introduction

If you're currently looking for work, here's some great news: The U.S. Bureau of Labor Statistics forecasts that total employment in the United States will rise by approximately 10 percent (that's 15.6 million jobs!) between 2006 and 2016 (source: *www.bls.gov*). This increase in job opportunities is accompanied by continuing changes in the composition of the workforce. Service-oriented industries such as healthcare, technology, engineering, transportation, social services, and others are growing at a rate of 20 percent during that same 10-year period, outdistancing goods-producing industries such as manufacturing and construction. These numbers indicate that it's actually a good time to be in the job market, whether you're a recent graduate, a worker in a skilled trade, a manager, an executive, or a veteran just transitioning from the military. The opportunities are numerous, but the challenge is to position yourself so that you grab the attention of prospective employers and land that great new job.

Job seekers often invest a great deal of time and effort (and sometimes money!) in preparing high-quality resumes and cover letters. Especially if you've had the chance to read *No-Nonsense Resumes* and *No-Nonsense Cover Letters* (both published by Career Press in 2006), you already understand the importance of these documents. No matter how worthy these documents may be, however, on their own they won't land you a job. It's only during the interview that you will be able to convince prospective employers of your unique value.

Once you have a dynamic, accomplishment-focused resume—and the powerful cover letters that complement it—and you've achieved the enviable goal of getting your documents in front of hiring decision-makers, the success of your job search now depends on how your performance in the interview is received by those decision-makers.

The quality of your interview performance will most certainly be shaped by how well you've prepared yourself. As important as a powerful resume and strong cover letter are to getting the interview, once you are granted an interview, you need to be ready to talk about your accomplishments in a way that convinces the employer that you are the right person for the job.

Job interviews have changed dramatically in recent years. The structure of interviews and the questions that are asked are designed to drill deeply into your personality and behavior, not just your job qualifications. It can cost an employer thousands of dollars to recruit, hire, and train a good employee. As a result, many employers have adopted a more rigorous approach to selecting and hiring employees, which may include a more in-depth interviewing process.

If you follow the strategies, steps, and activities contained in these pages, you'll be able to present the very best you in a wide variety of interview situations. You'll gain an awareness of a broad array of interviewing techniques, and an understanding of the interviewer's intent behind many of the questions asked. This will enable you to prepare answers that reflect your strengths and are optimally responsive to the employer's needs. You'll also come away with a fuller understanding of the entire interview process, which starts long before you find yourself sitting in front of an interviewer and lasts well beyond the good-bye handshake. You'll learn about the three Ps of job interviews: **preparation**, **presentation**, and **post-interview follow-up**. Finally, you'll find tips from esteemed colleagues who coach candidates preparing for job interviews. Their insights and valuable advice on how to address a variety of key issues appear in each chapter.

After reading this book, you should have a practical understanding of how to prepare for your job interviews, present yourself in a professional and compelling way, and conduct the all-important post-interview follow-up—all of which are necessary to give yourself a significant advantage over similarly qualified competitors, to be successful in the job interview process, and, ultimately, to land a great job in a field you enjoy.

Chapter 1

▶ Simple Truths About Job Interviews

Professional resume writers will tell you that a strong resume and cover letter will paint a compelling picture of how your unique skills can solve a prospective employer's challenges. Likewise, professional career coaches will tell you that a job interview is your opportunity to connect with the prospective employer, both on a professional and personal level, to sell your skills and abilities and, equally important, to determine if you believe there will be a good fit—in other words, to help you decide if you really want the job.

Many job seekers invest a great deal of energy and effort in developing resumes and cover letters. Countless books have been written on the topic (including a few by this author), and these documents are vitally important. In the final analysis, though, your cover letter and resume are actually all about winning you the opportunity to interview. Once you're there, how you present yourself and how well you connect with the interviewer(s) will determine whether you are invited back for a second interview and, ultimately, whether you are offered a job.

The Many Types of Job Interviews

Let's look at the hiring process from the employer's point of view for a moment. The costs associated with recruiting and retaining good people continue to escalate in this increasingly competitive marketplace. As a result, just as job seekers invest in resumes, cover letters, and search strategies, many employers invest in a variety of interview approaches, which they believe will most effectively identify candidates who will both fulfill the responsibilities of the position in question and be a good fit for their organization.

Hiring companies use a wide array of interview techniques to accomplish varying objectives. Here's a quick summary of some of the most common:

Types of Job Interviews

The Traditional	You're interviewed by the hiring decision-maker who also happens to be the person who would be your direct supervisor.
The Intermediary	You are interviewed by a representative of the HR department who may or may not be familiar with the position for which you are applying—and may be screening for follow-up interviews with the hiring authority.
Tasks and Challenges	You're presented with a specific task, such as prioritizing numerous items in an in-basket or solving a series of puzzles, and are evaluated on your judgment, creativity, and efficiency in completing the task.
Meet and Greet	You spend an entire day meeting individually or in small groups with various key stakeholders; this often includes meals and facility tours.
Firing Line	You're interviewed and evaluated by the members of a panel.
Sink or Swim	You're one of a group of candidates interviewed in the same space at the same time.
Groupthink	You're one of a small group of candidates who are asked to discuss an issue or solve a problem together—and are evaluated throughout the process.
Showtime	You're asked to prepare and deliver a presentation on a particular topic to key stakeholders—for example, how you would overcome a challenge the organization currently faces.
Remote Control	You're asked to go to a video conference site and are interviewed remotely by one or more people (the session will most likely be recorded).
Classic Good Cop/ Bad Cop	Two interviewers question you, with one behaving in a very engaging and friendly manner while the other is cold and aggressive.
Minute Waltz	Similar to speed dating, you get 15 minutes with the interviewer to make an impression. Currently popular for screening a large number of candidates for entry-level opportunities.
Problem Solved	You're given a word problem to solve. Typically, it's not about math skills, but about logic and the ability to work through the process to a solution.
Let's Do Lunch	You're interviewed by one or more stakeholders over breakfast, lunch, or dinner, and suddenly, it's all about the food and beverage and which fork to use.
Can You Hear Me Now?	You're interviewed by one or more people over the telephone.

Some information from this table adapted from material used in the Certified Employment Interview Coach (CEIC) training program offered by Career Directors International, as well as from *Interviewing: The Gold Standard*, by Laura DeCarlo. Used with permission.

In addition, some organizations include other surveys or so-called assessment tools, many of which are written or computer-based tests that probe and measure everything and anything imaginable that's legal to probe and measure (and some things that are not!). For example, these tests are designed to evaluate your aptitude in various disciplines (such as math, reading comprehension, and so on); identify your personality characteristics (for example, whether you are a team player or an individual contributor); and determine your level of expertise in a particular profession. In Chapter 6, many types of interviews will be explored in more depth to give you a better understanding of the interviewers' motives, the unique challenges presented, and how you can best prepare for these scenarios.

The 3 Ps of Job Interviewing

The job interview process begins long before you find yourself sitting in front of an interviewer, and lasts well beyond the end of that initial meeting. Recognizing this fact and understanding the steps in the process will put you well on your way to making a winning impression and landing that job offer. The three phases of the job interview process, what I call the 3 Ps, are preparation, presentation, and post-interview follow-up.

1. Preparation

Job seeker, know thyself

Before walking into an interview, it's absolutely vital for you to know not only your work history, but also your resume, inside and out. Whether you wrote it yourself or worked with a resume-writing professional, you should be familiar with and comfortable speaking about every detail of your resume. Be prepared to tell at least one story about every position and achievement noted on your resume. Ideally, each story should illustrate a particular skill or strength that is relevant to the target position. If you've done a good job of researching the company, you should have some ideas about what's important to the prospective employer, and then be able to connect that to the information on your resume.

Know your target

As you launch your job search and start sending your resume to prospective employers and/or recruiters, you should already be thinking about interview preparation. Presumably, you're sending your resume to organizations you'd like to work for. It's vital for you to thoroughly research those entities, as well as the specific positions you're applying for. Ideally, your findings will help you even before you contact a target employer to ensure that you truly wish to work there.

Don't be afraid to ask (or, forewarned is forearmed)

Recognize that from the moment you initiate contact with a target employer, the interview process has started. If your cover letter and resume have successfully opened the door for you, then expect a phone call or an e-mail message inviting you for the interview. Be mindful that as you respond to these initial communications, it's likely that evaluation of your candidacy is already fully underway. Know that as soon as you send out your first job inquiry, each time the phone rings, it could be your target employer or representative. What does this mean? If you have an especially humorous or bawdy voice mail message, consider modifying it—at least for the duration of your job search. If young children in the household sometimes answer the phone, it may be time for a quick refresher on proper phone manners and procedures. If you've provided your cellular phone number, consider whether it's wise to answer the phone at a sporting event or in a crowded, loud shopping mall—and then remember to check voice mail frequently and regularly!

Let's assume you receive a phone call inviting you to an interview. It is perfectly acceptable during this conversation for you to inquire about the type of interview and who will be meeting with you. There's nothing quite like anticipating a pleasant chat with the person who phoned you to schedule the appointment, only to find yourself walking into a large conference room with an eight-member panel prepared to fire questions at you.

Who knows you?

Another aspect of effective interview preparation is lining up a set of excellent professional references. To avoid any surprises that could hurt your chances with the potential employer, it's wise to contact your prospective references in advance to seek their permission. This communication will also create the opportunity for you to brief these folks on your job-search goals and ensure that you have their current contact information.

It's all about logistics

Another important aspect of preparation is planning for the logistics associated with job interviews. These include getting there (where is the interview taking place? Are you driving, riding the bus, or taking a taxi? What about the parking?); wardrobe and grooming decisions (what's most appropriate to wear? Should you get a haircut?); and deciding what to take with you (recent performance appraisals? Formal letters of reference? College transcripts? Your professional portfolio?). And, by the way, do you practice the four components of a good handshake? Do you even know what they are?

2. Presentation

Taking the show on the road

Once you've done your research on the prospective employer, lined up a set of superb references, selected your wardrobe, and planned how to get yourself to the meeting, it's showtime! Now you need to be ready for the actual interview. Hopefully, you now know what the format will be, who will conduct it, and if anyone else will be present (think back to the types of interviews mentioned previously). Your thorough research will have provided some insights into the culture and the management philosophy you will encounter. The more knowledge you have about what to expect, the less surprised you will be on the day of the interview.

Section II addresses in further detail the different types of interviews and what to expect from each. Each of these interview types has an underlying purpose, and prospective employers will choose a particular type because they believe it will meet their needs. Knowing what that purpose is can help you tailor your interview preparation so that you put your best foot forward.

What's the question?

Regardless of which interview format you are presented with, there are certain questions you can expect to be asked in just about any interview. Be mindful that although these may seem routine, there's still plenty of room to be tripped up if you don't thoroughly prepare your remarks in advance. Likewise, there are several common tough questions that you should anticipate. These will vary depending on the target position and your particular work history. For example, such questions could probe gaps in employment or dismissal from a job, or focus on why you're looking to change careers, move laterally, or take a job that might appear to be a downward move. Whatever the circumstances, these questions can easily trip you up, so you need to be ready to answer them honestly.

It goes both ways

Being prepared to ask your own questions at the interview is just as important as being prepared to answer the interviewer's questions. This can be your opportunity to gain further insights into the requirements for the position, why the position is vacant, and what the opportunities for advancement may be. Inquiries along these lines will help you to better understand if this organization and job situation are right for you. Asking thoughtful questions can subtly communicate to the interviewer that you are envisioning your future as a long-term employee, and can demonstrate your serious interest in the organization, both of which will enhance your credibility as a candidate.

One very important piece of information to find out during the interview has to do with timing. If the information isn't volunteered, it is acceptable for you to ask what the timetable is for the hiring decision, and when it would be appropriate for you to follow up.

It's not all about the money!

The one question you *don't* want to ask in an initial interview is the salary question. Talking about salary in a job interview is akin to a game of chicken: whoever turns—or in this case, speaks—first is in a weaker position. That is to say, whoever mentions a dollar figure first is at a decided disadvantage in any subsequent negotiations. It's very easy to fall into this trap, especially if an interviewer pointedly asks what your salary expectations are.

When you encounter a premature salary discussion, the secret is to refocus the conversation—perhaps by asking a question of your own, such as "Well, what kind of range do you have in mind for the position?" Better yet, defer the discussion of salary by saying, "I'm sure that if we can agree that I'm the right person for the job and that I'll be a good fit within your organization, the salary will be in line with the responsibilities of the position." This may sound simple and straightforward, but of course it's not so easy when you're in the hot seat.

Take names

During the interview, make sure that you note the names and job titles of the people who conduct the interview, and anyone else you meet during your visit. The easiest approach is to ask for business cards from each person you meet, whether you meet one or 18. If you forget to ask for business cards or are unable to jot down the information, it's a good idea to call back and speak with the receptionist or other support staff to confirm names or check on correct spellings. You may also be able to find the information you need on the employer's Website.

3. Post-interview follow-up

It is after the interview ends that perhaps the most important phase of the process begins. Diligent post-interview follow-up can solidify your position as a leading candidate for the job, keep your name in front of the interviewer(s)/decision-makers so that you're top-of-mind, and sometimes even salvage your candidacy if you believe things went poorly during the interview.

Self-evaluation

First, honestly evaluate your performance. Overall, how do you think you did in the interview? Which questions did you answer well? Which questions could you have answered more effectively? Are you disappointed in some of the answers the interviewer gave in response to your own questions? Honestly and objectively appraising your performance as well as the interviewer's will help to gauge how you should conduct your follow-up.

Thank you very much

A thank-you letter can be the tiebreaker in a close race with another well-qualified candidate, or it can rescue your candidacy if things went poorly. If you believe the interview went well, the thank-you letter can be used to further strengthen your candidacy by reinforcing key points that came out in the interview, or by introducing relevant facts that were not already mentioned in the interview.

If you truly feel that the interview went poorly, or if you missed an opportunity to make an important point, the thank-you letter is your chance to correct the record. Perhaps on the way home from the interview you suddenly remember a great example of how you overcame a particular challenge that completely slipped your mind during the interview. Maybe you realize you neglected to mention that you did, in fact, attend a three-day training session on a key software application that is relevant to the new job. This letter is your opportunity to convey your message precisely as you wish you had expressed it during the interview. Furthermore, armed with the new information you learned during your visit, you can develop a follow-up letter that addresses some of the prospective employer's challenges, and shows specifically how your capabilities are poised to meet those challenges.

Should you decide at this point that you no longer wish to pursue the opportunity further, it's perfectly acceptable to write a simple letter thanking the interviewer for his or her time and respectfully asking that your name be withdrawn from further consideration.

It's vital for you to send follow-up correspondence as soon as possible after an interview. Ideally, you should get a letter in the mail the same day, or the next day at the very latest. It can be a formally typed letter mailed in a business envelope, a hand-written note card, or an e-mail message. The key here is to have a sense of the organization's culture as well as the time frame for the hiring decision. If your target is a high-tech company where everyone uses Bluetooth technology and BlackBerry devices, an e-mail message may be appropriate. If your target is a "boutique" organization that values camaraderie and personal interactions, the hand-written note is most likely the best choice. Most employers will fall somewhere in the middle, in which case a typed letter is appropriate.

Following the initial follow-up

Hopefully, during the interview, you were able to learn the timetable for the hiring decision, and when it would be appropriate for you to make a follow-up inquiry. Let's say the interviewer indicated three weeks; sometime during week three, you'll want to contact that person to see if there's any other information you should provide.

If you haven't heard by the middle of week four, maybe the final decision has been delayed. Consider sending a follow-up letter or e-mail message reminding the interviewer of your meeting and your continuing interest in the position.

In many instances, the first interview is for screening purposes, and will lead to a second interview if you make the cut. This second interview will probably be with a higher-level decision-maker, your prospective supervisor, and/or one or more other people in the department in which you would be working. Second interviews differ somewhat from first interviews in terms of substance, but many of the same rules apply for preparation and presentation.

Summary

Any time two people interact with each other, especially if it's for the first time, both parties are trying, consciously and subconsciously, to assess the verbal and non-verbal cues in order to determine what they should do or say next. In the job interview game, the prospective employer is seeking to identify the best qualified person for the position, while the candidate is striving to make a favorable impression that will result in a job offer. Both players bring unique "baggage" to the meeting, and both wish to avoid making a mistake. The prospective employer can make a mistake by choosing the wrong person for the job (either someone who is unqualified or who is not a good fit), or, conversely, by ruling out the "perfect" candidate. From the other side of the table, the candidate can erroneously conclude the position is no longer desirable, or can suffer from a case of high anxiety, which results in being deselected based on a poor performance in the interview.

By understanding and following the 3 Ps of job interviewing, you can make a favorable and compelling impression on hiring decision-makers and give yourself an advantage over similarly qualified candidates. Ultimately, this should significantly help you land a job you love with an organization that values your contribution.

Part 1

▶ Preparation

Chapter 2

▶ Simple Truths About Your Resume and the Job Interview

Your ultimate goal is to arrive at a mutually beneficial employment agreement with your prospective employer, one that fairly compensates you for working in a job that will bring you personal fulfillment. Our no-nonsense approach to achieving this goal calls for you to:

- ▶ Know yourself and your resume, inside and out.
- ▶ Become as familiar as humanly possible with your prospective employer.
- ▶ Match your qualifications with the target position requirements.
- ▶ Identify the unique value you offer the prospective employer.
- ▶ Develop relevant success stories that demonstrate your value to your target employer.

The job interview is your golden opportunity to convince the hiring decision-makers that you will exceed their expectations. Let's proceed with preparing you to do just that, and more.

Job Seeker, Know Thyself

Success is getting what you want. Happiness is wanting what you get.

–Anonymous

A truer statement was perhaps never written. Let's consider a few deceptively simple questions: Who are you and what do you really want? Viewed from another perspective, if you gain the whole world and lose your soul, have you really won? Whatever your answer may be, I humbly recommend that you make a commitment to yourself that you will continue to do what it takes to discover, create, and pursue career choices that optimally fit your unique personal values, capabilities, and aspirations. *Be true to yourself.* Can you make that promise?

It is vital for you to review each word and every interpretation of the materials in your resume and other job-search correspondence. This is particularly important if you have benefited from the assistance of someone else in preparing your job-search documents. You must be intimately familiar with absolutely every experience noted on your resume and be prepared to comfortably discuss even those things that may seem trivial or unrelated to the target position. Prepare yourself as though you were going to take an exam, and the study material is your own work history. Every item on your resume is open to scrutiny and probing questions. Practice answering inquiries about every job you've held, each accomplishment listed, and every educational experience you've noted. Really know your resume, inside and out.

No matter how friendly, engaging, or informal the interviewer may seem, being authentic (true to yourself) in a job interview does not mean that you are required to confess mistakes or imperfections unrelated to job performance, or to speak ill of prior or current employers (or of anyone!). After all, it's the interviewer's job to get you to let your guard down and reveal information that you may not want to reveal. Likewise, presenting the best you in a job interview doesn't translate to behaving in an artificial manner or pretending to be some idealized version of yourself, nor does it mean that it's ever acceptable to state falsehoods.

Tips From the Pros

Think of your resume as a marketing document—your personal advertisement with you as the featured product! You need to be able to provide the back-up detail on any point highlighted in your personal advertisement. The impression of false or misleading advertising can be avoided by thorough preparation by you in advance of the interview.

Laurie Berenson, CPRW

Sterling Career Concepts, LLC

Many interviewers will use your resume as a guide throughout the interview process. For example, the interviewer may read a sentence from an achievement noted on your resume and ask you to elaborate. If you are not adequately familiar with your resume, fumble your way through your response, or otherwise appear flustered, the interviewer may view you as unprofessional or even be skeptical of the truth of what's contained in your resume. Review the information on your resume many times before attending interviews. Revisit your work experiences to gain a fresh understanding of the details that may be hard to recall with clarity to help you answer related questions with confidence.

Kris Plantrich, CPRW, CEIP

Resume Wonders

Become an expert in interviewing yourself! Read and re-read your resume from top to bottom to familiarize yourself with every line. Anything on your resume is fair game for a question during an interview. Don't try to second-guess which items may catch an interviewer's attention.

Laurie Berenson, CPRW

Sterling Career Concepts, LLC

Keep in mind that responsibility for the content of your resume remains yours, even though you may have sought help from books, Websites, friends, relatives, or professional writers. When asked to elaborate on some point contained in your resume, refrain—at all costs—from blurting out something like, "Someone else helped me write this resume, and that's not what I really meant to say!" It's a quick way to lose credibility with the interviewer, and prove again that time spent reviewing your job search documents before the interview is a priceless investment.

Melanie Noonan

Peripheral Pro

Remember to thoroughly review the details "behind" anything mentioned on your resume. You may find it helpful to write out this additional information separately and review it before each interview.

Laurie Berenson, CPRW

Sterling Career Concepts, LLC

Be sure to keep a copy of the resume you sent along with the job posting in a safe place for future reference. Remember that weeks or even months may pass before you actually participate in an interview with a particular employer. In the meantime, you may have revised your resume, perhaps even more than once. You may have added, re-framed, or deleted some or much of the content. If an interviewer asks a question about something that you have since deleted, it could be an opportunity for you to appear unnecessarily confused or uncertain during your response, and create an embarrassing and unfavorable impression—one that was completely preventable! It's vital that you are intimately familiar with the version of the resume that you originally sent to the prospective employer.

Norine Dagliano, NCRW, CPRW, CFRW/CC

ekm Inspirations

Focus on Your Target: Research!

Another way to favorably distinguish yourself from other similarly qualified candidates is to know more about the target employer than your competition does. When the field is narrowed to two or three fairly evenly matched, well-qualified job seekers, each with comparable skills and experience, can you understand how the scales may well tip in favor of the person who has demonstrated a genuine interest in the target employer by being just that much more prepared and engaged in the process? Research can make the difference!

Many hiring decision-makers also consider research a reflection of a candidate's intelligence, his or her commitment to career, and his or her work ethic—all favorable characteristics that will help set you apart from your competition. An added bonus is that you'll naturally feel more confident at the interview; after all, the notion that knowledge is power has a basis in fact—no nonsense! On the other side of the coin, it may turn out that your research uncovers information that helps you decide that you would prefer not to pursue opportunities with this employer. If so, invest your valuable time and energy in discovering other opportunities that more closely align with your search criteria.

In general, the higher the level or the greater the measure of responsibility associated with the target position, the more extensive your research needs to be. Following is a list of areas to focus on (this applies for positions in nonprofit organizations, too):

▶ General background: mission and vision, length of time in business, and so on.

▶ Key products and services: challenges and opportunities.

▶ Current issues or events: new developments, mergers, acquisitions, and so on.

▶ Major competitors: rivalries, price pressure, and service innovations.

▶ Organizational structure: key decision-makers, outside contractors, and so on.

> ▶ Corporate culture: the day-to-day "climate" and dress code.

> ▶ Target position description: what does the prospective employer need?

If you're Internet savvy, you should be able to learn a great deal about your target employer(s). You'll want to start by exploring the employer's official Website and any blogs. There may also be a wealth of information available on the Internet beyond the employer's own Website. Consider visiting a library online; many major libraries have online or telephone reference services available. Be on the lookout for current information on the employer's customers or clients, recent successes or failures, and any related news stories. If your target employer is not local, remember to search newspapers in the target community, as well. If your target is a publicly traded company, the most recent annual report will provide a great deal of good information (there are resources available to help you translate and interpret "annual report–speak"). There are also fee-based services that will conduct research on your behalf and provide you with a comprehensive report, often on short notice. Appendix C offers a list of favorite research resources recommended by the esteemed experts who have contributed the tips you see throughout this book. If you're not comfortable traveling the information superhighway, a wealth of information can be found through your local library or Chamber of Commerce. Professional library staff can be a tremendous resource. If you live in a remote area, you may need to contact a library in the nearest city.

What is the corporate culture of your target employer? "Corporate culture" generally refers to what the "feel" and pace of the workplace is like. For example, is the workplace laid back? Dynamic? Frantic? Casual and informal? Internally competitive? Structured and hierarchical? Contentious and aggressive? Highly sophisticated? What you learn about an organization's culture may be a critical factor in determining how well you will fit in. You may discover a few clues to the culture in some of the resources mentioned in Appendix C; some organizations even post their human resources policy manuals, along with job postings and position descriptions, on their Websites.

Because exploring and assessing an organization's culture is a subjective process, "softer" sources may be more beneficial here. As part of your overall job-search strategy, you likely will have already activated your own professional network of contacts; use it wisely! Consider attending local or regional meetings of professional trade associations or related organizations. These events may provide you the opportunity to further refine your networking skills and learn valuable information about your chosen field and target employers. Additionally, professional associations or other membership groups related to your field may have online chat spaces, e-bulletin boards, or other electronic venues that can offer helpful information. This is another area in which it is perfectly acceptable to request assistance from public library staff.

Pick up a notebook and begin to record your findings. Depending on your particular job search, some of the sources suggested here will be more or less relevant; or, you may discover other sources that are even more important in your particular field. You may also notice patterns and trends in your chosen field as you research more than one prospective employer. Remember: The more highly competitive the hiring situation, the more vital it will be for you to be as knowledgeable as you can possibly be when you interview. How you apply your research could make the difference in whether you are offered the job.

Tips From the Pros

The easiest way to begin researching your prospective employer is to get on the Internet! What meaningful attributes are most important to you in your next employer? Visit the Website, and read as much as you can to see to what extent the organization's values align with your own. Are they "going green?" Do they have a heart for children? For education? How important is healthcare to them? Fully explore the Website; remember to check out their press releases; read as much as you can, and determine if there is a good match. You will probably work best in an organization where you feel most comfortable, where there is a good "fit" and where the environment is most conducive to your needs and values.

Makini Theresa Harvey, CPRW, JCTC, CEIP, CCM

Career Abundance

Imagine the interviewer challenging you with this question: "What do you know about my company?" Now, imagine being asked that question, and calmly pulling out a three-ring presentation binder that contains a complete dossier on the company. You can create such a presentation by inserting a full-page cover sheet in the front sleeve featuring the employer's logo and name, and similarly prominently label the spine. Then, inside the binder, include printouts of key sections of the employer's Website and/or annual report and other relevant information (press clippings, etc.). Take the time to tab/highlight particularly key points. Even if you're not directly asked during the interview, find a reason to open this binder and refer to a particular point that you have highlighted. The fact that you made the effort to research the employer speaks volumes about your abilities, as well as your thoroughness and desire to perform well. It will knock their socks off!

Dawn L. Rasmussen, CTP, CMP

Pathfinder Writing and Career Services, LLC

Recruiters tell me that candidates who haven't visited the employer's Website are usually automatically excluded from further consideration. It's even more powerful to take your research beyond the employer's Website. For example, while at the official Website, look for names of the individuals who run the organization. Then, separately Google them. From the organization's own Website, learn the names of products and/or services offered. Then, separately Google them, too. Learn what's been happening from official press releases on the organization's Website (new products, new contacts, new clients, personnel announcements, etc.). Conduct separate Google searches as viable, to learn even more. For example, it may be wise to beware of the abrupt departure of a senior executive or negative news stories about a company's product.

Susan P. Joyce

Editor/Webmaster since 1998

Remember that you are also interviewing the prospective employer to assess whether it and the position are a good fit for you. It's perfectly acceptable to contact the prospective employer prior to the interview to request details on the position you're pursuing as well as company literature. Your research also helps greatly if the interviewer should ask, "Why do you want to work here?" Knowing as much as possible about the organization and its future plans can make your interview far more interactive, and could be the boost you need.

Doris Appelbaum, BA, MS

Appelbaum's Resume Professionals, Inc.

Make the Connections

Hopefully, your focused and extensive research has yielded some beyond-the-basics background about the prospective employer, along with a job description for your target position. Here's where elements of what we've discussed so far converge: Examine your skills, abilities, education, training, and experience *specifically within the context of the expectations for your target position*; that is to say, view your qualifications through the prism of what the target employer needs.

To optimally demonstrate to the interviewer that you are perfect for the position, it's vital to express your value in terms of the benefit you offer, rather than simply recount your qualifications. Clearly, your credentials and qualifications are important. However, to distinguish yourself from the competition—all of whom may be similarly qualified—it's essential to translate your qualifications into meaningful benefits beyond simple listings of skills and credentials. Paint a picture for the interviewer, showing the relevant value that you bring to the table that specifically addresses the employer's needs.

Use the following worksheet as a guide to help organize your thoughts. Have a copy of your resume along with the target job description available as you list and evaluate your qualifications. In fact, as I discussed in *No-Nonsense Cover Letters*, this approach also can be highly effective in developing cover letters that introduce your resume and powerfully express your value to the prospective employer.

Value Inventory Worksheet

Position Requirements (From Job Description)	My Qualifications (From Your Resume)	Benefits I Offer (Value I Bring)
Minimum of two years of experience in customer-service role at call center.	Five years of experience with Northumberland Consolidated Care, four in call center.	As a certified CSR instructor, I can train other employees on the most effective techniques in dealing with customers who have serious issues and concerns. This improves customer satisfaction, reduces the number of escalated customer issues, and, ultimately, leads to enhanced customer loyalty.
Pleasant telephone personality.	Friendly, engaging manner. Maintain composure and professionalism in all situations.	Able to help customers feel at ease, and quickly establish positive rapport on the telephone with even the most irate callers, thus encouraging continued business relationship.

First, fill in the position requirements column based upon the target job description. If you weren't able to come up with the actual job description from your prospective employer, try searching online for similar positions with other employers to use in your preparation.

Next, examine your own background and skill set for elements that directly address the employer's needs, and enter them in column two of the worksheet. This document is for your eyes only, so feel free to make notes as necessary (for example, to remind you of skills that you may not have been using in your current position).

Now it's time to move beyond the ordinary. Identify your value in terms of the benefit you offer that directly addresses the prospective employer's needs, rather than by merely recounting your qualifications. Review the results of your research, and examine the position description with these questions in mind:

▶ How can you solve a specific problem the employer is encountering?

▶ How can you contribute to increasing the employer's profitability? Can you reduce expenses or grow revenue?

▶ How can you enhance the efficiency of operations? Can you make process improvements which may save time and ultimately reduce expenses or grow revenue?

▶ How can you attract more clients or enhance client retention? Can you cold call, or build relationships, as demonstrated by sales performance in previous jobs?

In addition to giving you a clear sense of how qualified you may be to meet or exceed the employer's expectations, completing this exercise also provides the building blocks for creating success stories that will illustrate how perfect you are for your target position.

Moving Up: Your Elevator Speech

Everybody engaged in a job search needs an "elevator speech." This is a brief introduction that you always have ready when some asks, "So, tell me about yourself...." It is most useful in networking situations but can also be a useful tool in the interview. The name comes from the fact that an average elevator ride lasts one to two minutes. If you had that brief opportunity to explain to a stranger on the elevator who you are and what you are about, you would give them your elevator speech.

In the context of a job interview, your elevator speech can be your answer to the "tell me about yourself" question when asked by the interviewer, and can serve as a lead-in to talking about your professional portfolio and how your qualifications address the employer's needs.

You should write the speech (it should be about one typewritten, double-spaced page), and then practice it until it's second nature and you can deliver it smoothly and naturally without sounding contrived or overly rehearsed.

Here's an example:

Hi, I'm Rosalyn Nottingham. My expertise is helping not-for-profit organizations prepare to successfully navigate the challenges ahead, especially in the areas of funding, technology, and staff development. I offer 15 years of experience in senior leadership roles with multi-million dollar not-for-profits that receive funding from state and local governments, as well as federal grants and private sources. Serving on a wide range of advisory boards at the state and national level has further broadened my strong understanding of the challenges faced by not-for-profit entities. My strengths include:

▶ *Establishing strategic vision.*

▶ *Community outreach.*

▶ *Developing and managing budgets.*

▶ *Dealing with funding sources.*

▶ *Managing capital projects.*

▶ *Influencing decision-makers.*

▶ *Implementing technology plans.*

▶ *Building and motivating teams.*

▶ *Leading PR initiatives.*

▶ *Developing and mentoring staff.*

I bring a dynamic energy and genuine enthusiasm to the role of leader, and set an upbeat, positive tone, even under highly challenging circumstances. I believe the potential exists for growth beyond survival, where the organization can fulfill its mission as it thrives and flourishes.

Develop Success Stories: It's All About You—Except That It's Not!

What is a success story? It's an absolutely truthful tale that illustrates your value to an employer. If you've read *No-Nonsense Cover Letters* and *No-Nonsense Resumes*, you've already been introduced to the concept of writing forward and focusing your resume on the target position. Along these lines, the best success stories connect with the employer's need, and demonstrate how you've done it before and you can do it again. The key is for the "it" to be directly relevant to the employer. Like most good stories, the most successful success stories contain a beginning, a middle, and ending— preferably an impressive, dynamite one. Careers professionals refer to these elements in a variety of meaningful ways, including PAR (problem, action, and resolution); STAR (situation/task, action, and result); or my personal favorite, CAR (challenge, action, and result).

The **challenge** in CAR is a situation you encountered or a task you were assigned. Describe the circumstances and the context. Be sure to include a few quantitative details—enough to make the story meaningful but not so many particulars that it will be overwhelming and shift the focus from the primary objective of the story.

The **action** is what you did to overcome the challenge, resolve the conflict or issue, solve the problem, or otherwise snatch victory from the jaws of defeat. Be sure to include how you approached the situation, and what your decision-making process was in determining what action to take. Also note whether this was an individual or team effort. If you were a member of a team, describe your role and how you interacted with other team members.

The **result** is the outcome achieved through your actions. This is also your opportunity to ensure that your relevance will be obvious to your prospective employer. Consider the outcome in terms of benefits derived not only for your work group, but for your department, your organization, your organization's clients, and perhaps even your industry or your community. It's vital to be as quantitative as possible here, and perhaps draw comparisons to a variety of benchmarks, such as the organization's past record, the industry's standard or average, or a competitor's known performance.

Let's see how a compelling and relevant success story can set you apart from the competition. Here's an example that one of my clients, Serena, shared when she called to report that she aced her interview and accepted a great job offer: She was applying for an executive assistant position for the COO of a pharmaceutical firm. Serena had done her homework. The position description emphasized the fact that they needed someone who was highly organized. Not surprisingly, the interviewer asked her how she had handled an extremely challenging situation in her current position, and wanted to know how organized she really was.

It turns out that in her previous position, Serena was an administrative assistant for the manager of a financial services agency. Due to the firm's rapid growth, it occupied space on both the 23rd and 24th floors of a downtown skyscraper. When prime space in a nearby office building became available that would allow consolidation of everyone into one large suite, the agency manager selected Serena to manage the relocation. She developed a success story that encompassed details (just enough, not too many) of the complexity of this project, and adapted the story to demonstrate her highly sophisticated planning and detail management skills that she brought to bear in orchestrating this major move on time and under budget.

The punch line? Another piece of intelligence uncovered by Serena's research was that her target employer was also anticipating the need to relocate within the same city during the next fiscal year. Armed with this knowledge, Serena was able to carefully prepare herself to fully capitalize on her prior experience in relocating with another company. A very successful success story!

The best success stories clearly show how you have already succeeded in analogous circumstances, and demonstrate to the target employer how you have the transferable knowledge, skills, and motivation to meet their needs and exceed expectations in the position. Notice that, at first glance, Serena's experience working for a financial services agency doesn't appear to make her a sought-after candidate to support a pharmaceutical executive. However, her completed value inventory worksheet illustrated that, in fact, she already possessed the skills and abilities necessary to excel in her target position. She was able to describe her accomplishments and effectively show that the underlying skills were highly transferable to the target position. She connected her abilities—as demonstrated by her accomplishments (knowing herself)—to the employer's needs and challenges (learned from her research sources).

In Serena's case, she noted that relocation consisted of 24 individual offices plus administrative support work areas, for a total of 36 employees. She also noted the square footage of office space, as well as the fact that she completed the project 8 percent under budget. She was especially proud of the fact that business as usual was conducted on the Friday before the move: She coordinated the professional movers on Saturday and Sunday, and by Monday morning, each employee's office was fully equipped for action, with telephones and computers reconnected and ready for business once again—one half-day ahead of schedule.

How is success measured for your target position? This can vary depending upon your field, as well as the particular position within that field. For example, in the world of sales, success may be measured dramatically differently than it is for teachers—or nurses, or IT professionals. Whatever your field, reexamine the position description, and once you have developed several different success stories, classify them according to the primary value or competency you offer that is illustrated in each story. It's wise to cover several different competency areas. Remember, as you develop your stories to highlight your various skills, abilities, and strengths, the guiding principle is to be mindful of the employer's needs and the requirements stated for the target position. To spark your thinking, here are just a few examples of possible categories for your success stories:

▶ Do you have exceptional written and verbal communication skills? Are you a gifted public speaker? An extraordinary cold-caller?

▶ Are you skilled at conflict resolution among coworkers, disgruntled clients, and/or the public?

▶ Are you media savvy? Are you skilled in handling delicate PR issues or potential fiascos? Are you comfortable handling print and/or electronic media?

▶ Are you skilled in customer focus? Do you have exceptional customer advocacy and/or client relations skills?

▶ Do you have exceptional social skills, as demonstrated by your discretion, diplomacy, and composure under fire?

▶ Are you a quick learner? Can you learn new software under severe time constraints?

▶ Are you persuasive? Are you a natural salesperson or advocate?

▶ Are you detail-oriented, yet still able to see the big picture while maintaining quality in complex operations?

▶ Are you an efficiency enhancer? Are you an innovator who suggests improvements that streamline operations?

> ▸ Are you a cost reducer? Do you have a successful track record of accomplishing more with less?

> ▸ Are you an outside-the-box thinker? Do you develop creative solutions?

Here's another example of a success story made relevant to an employment opportunity: Bob applied for a marketing position with a firm that was about to launch a new product. His last position was as a district sales manager for a beverage company that introduced a new energy drink. Bob increased sales from virtually nil (500 cases per month) to an average of 50,000 cases per month in less than 18 months. He was so successful that the company was sold to a major international beverage company and he was out of a job. When relating this story to his prospective new employer, he highlighted how he was able to recruit a crack team of enthusiastic, recent college graduates to implement a statewide product sampling campaign, develop promotional partnerships with key radio and TV outlets in the various key markets, and work with channel partners (distributors) to get the product onto store shelves. All of these skills were relevant to the new product launch that the target employer was anticipating, and Bob put himself in the lead among candidates for the new position.

Yet another example is Ted, who was a project manager for a construction company. A typical project could last 18 to 36 months and in that business, cost overruns and delays were so common that they were considered the norm. By contrast, Ted had built a reputation for completing projects on time and under budget. He was able to show how he had used innovative approaches and team-building skills in order to work efficiently and gain cooperation from subcontractors in meeting ambitious goals. By beating the established timelines, Ted made his employer eligible for performance incentives that made the project even more profitable and lucrative. By citing concrete examples of how much money he saved and how far ahead of schedule he was, Ted demonstrated to his prospective employer how he could bring value that would far exceed his annual salary. The new company was eager to hire him.

Now let's look at the world from the employer's perspective for a moment. A new hire represents a tremendous investment of resources by the employer: non-productive time spent waiting for a new employee; staff time spent recruiting, interviewing, training, and more; the costs of travel, training materials, instructors, salary, medical benefits, insurances, taxes, and more; and that old intangible, opportunity cost (which means that the same resources could be invested elsewhere).

A new hire also represents a significant risk to the employer; hiring the wrong person could damage a smoothly-running operation and ultimately cost the employer a valuable client relationship. It could also cause internal strife and turmoil such that production dramatically drops, or worse. Let's agree that the decision to hire a new employee is both a major investment and risk for the employer, analogous to the investment and risk faced by the candidate.

The employer's decision to seek new employees is fundamentally based on need. That is, the employer's decision-makers have concluded that current staff is insufficient or inadequate to face current or future challenges. Your goal is to demonstrate that you have everything it takes to meet these needs—now that you have identified them. An effective success story is a powerful tool in responding to interview questions and proving your value.

Tips From the Pros

Begin developing your success stories now! This process should really begin as soon as you start working, even as early as high school. A "Work Success Journal" is essential to record your accomplishments for use in seeking promotions or new positions. Ideally, begin a success journal on your very first day. Visit *www.jibberjobber.com* for guidance. The first page should be your job description so that you are absolutely clear about your responsibilities and expectations. You can easily compare your activities with how well you are handling tasks and meeting requirements. Set up a loose-leaf binder or portfolio with the job description in front, followed by these sections:

- My goals and objectives: what you want to achieve in this job.

- Performance appraisals: what your supervisors say about your work.

- Recognition and awards.

- Success stories: your accomplishments (express using CAR or similar method).

Consider bringing your Success Journal to the interview. Presenting your success stories will show your unique promise of value and make a great impression on the prospective employer.

Makini Theresa Harvey, CPRW, JCTC, CEIP, CCM

Career Abundance

It is important to remember when developing success stories that they must be relevant to the position you are seeking. Examples of earlier achievements are most helpful when they incorporate several skills the prospective job requires. Using the job vacancy announcement during preparation is a great way to ensure you demonstrate all the skills and behavior patterns sought for the position.

Kris Plantrich, CPRW, CEIP

Resume Wonders Writing and Career Coaching Services

A story format is the best way to demonstrate your skills and provide proof of performance. Behavioral interviewing, which is used by more than 30 percent of employers, offers the perfect venue for telling your success stories. First, understand the responsibilities required in the position. This will help you select the most appropriate stories to discuss. Keep in mind that answering behavioral interview questions requires both specific and complete stories that relate to the employer's needs and the job that you are hoping to fill.

Louise Garver, CPRW, MCDP, CMP, JCTC, CLBF, CPBS, CEIP, COIS

Career Directions, LLC

Everyone loves an easy choice, whether buying a gift for a friend or hiring an employee. If a candidate stands out during the interview process, an employer is often relieved and happy to be able to make a quick decision. Remember that interviewers are often uncomfortable during the interview, too; many probably have never received interview training. The stakes are high for them, too; if they recommend you, and you don't work out, they look bad, too. As human beings, they also want to be liked. They do not want to turn people away, and may be hesitant to tell you the truth if they are not satisfied. Seek details of the perfect hire's qualifications from the interviewer. Then make it easy to choose you by sharing the perfect stories.

Gail Frank, CPRW, NCRW, JCTC, CEIP, MA

Employment University

Using success stories in job interviews helps the interviewer to visualize you living up to your stated strengths. For example, an interviewer might ask, "What are your three best strengths?" A typical answer might be, "I'm reliable, get along well with coworkers, and learn quickly." To follow up on this brief answer, the candidate might add, "When I first started at my current job with Blue Mountain Framing, I needed to learn the company's software and be ready to use it on the sales floor the following week. It was different from anything I had previously used, but I have strong computer skills and was able to observe my coworkers between my other duties. I also stayed after my shift two nights to practice. By Monday morning, I was using the software proficiently with customers in a high-volume store." Besides illustrating the point that the candidate is a fast learner, a story like this one often reveals more skills or traits than you would be able to express in a more basic "skill list" response.

Heather Carson, CPRW, GCDF, JCTC

Second Start

Chapter 3

▶ **S**imple **T**ruths **A**bout
Your **R**eferences

References are a key component of your job search, one that many candidates frequently overlook. Once upon a time, references were almost an afterthought, listed at the end of a job application. Job seekers would use their neighbors, their in-laws, or their ministers on the premise that these folks would say good things about them if anyone ever called. And the truth is that, often, the references were never checked. If the interview went well, the offer was made and the applicant went to work.

In today's job market, things have changed dramatically. You've already read about how employers may spend thousands of dollars to recruit and retain good employees. As part of the ever-growing effort to ensure they are making wise choices, employers are more and more interested in what references have to say about you. Much more thought needs to be put into developing solid references that can advance your candidacy by speaking cogently and persuasively about your professional qualifications.

"Who Ya Gonna Call?"

In selecting your references, you want to choose people who know about your work history and can legitimately speak, with firsthand knowledge, about your capacity to perform the job you are targeting. This generally means that you will want to limit yourself to choosing former supervisors, coworkers, customers, and, in certain cases, subordinates who have worked with you and whom you are confident will have no problem speaking positively about you.

Unless a prospective employer asks specifically for personal references (also called character references), avoid using neighbors, relatives, or clergy people as job references. Anyone with the title of Reverend or Pastor in front of his or her name will be discounted by the employer as someone who will, by the nature of their office, only view you in the most positive light. A neighbor or relative who has no real knowledge of how you carry out your responsibilities at work can't credibly tell the employer in what ways you'll be an asset to the new company, thus discounting them as viable professional references. The only exception to this advice—and admittedly, it's a rare exception—is if you are personally acquainted with a high-profile public figure. If you live next door to the mayor, or your son plays on the same little league team as the CEO of a local company, listing them as a reference could be advantageous.

Think about your success stories that you developed in Chapter 2. Whom have you worked with or had regular business contact with who is aware of those successes? These are the people to consider using as references. Put together a list of potential references, keeping in mind their knowledge of your successes as well as your personal relationships with them. A former supervisor may have extensive knowledge of your performance, but if you didn't hit it off very well with each other, you may not feel comfortable asking her or him to be your reference. Is there a different supervisor that either preceded or succeeded this person, who has similar knowledge of your accomplishments? That person could be a better choice. Do you have a positive rapport with one of your former customers such that you would feel comfortable listing him or her as a reference?

A word of caution here: You don't want to jeopardize an existing business relationship for the sake of a job. It's generally accepted that people don't use their current employers as references while conducting a job search. Many candidates have been fired for looking for work while still employed. Recruiters and prospective employers understand this and, assuming they're ethical, won't ask you to do anything that would put your current position at risk. They may, however, ask permission to contact your current employer after you have been hired in order to verify your employment and any claims you may have made on your resume or application.

Are You Okay With That?

Never use someone as a reference without discussing the matter with her or him first! Once you've compiled a list of potential references, you should contact each of them and explain that you are conducting a job search. Ask permission to use his or her name as a reference. If letters of recommendation are offered, graciously accept them, but you and your references should understand that they will still likely be contacted by prospective employers. You should make an effort to have no less than three and perhaps as many as six or eight people lined up to serve as references. You'll also want to make sure that your references have copies of your resume, and that they understand what your current goals are. It may have been some time since you worked with some of these people, and your career path may have taken some turns since you were last in touch. Therefore, you want to bring each of them up to date on your current activities. Later in this chapter, advice about coaching your references is explored in more depth.

What's Your Number?

Once you've established who your references are, make sure you have accurate and up-to-date contact information for each of them. At the very minimum, you should have their names, daytime phone numbers, e-mail addresses, and their relationship to you. For example:

Mr. Chip Circuit

Chief Development Engineer

Macrosoft International

209-456-7890

Chip.circuit@macrosoft.us.com

Former Supervisor at Tangerine Systems

(*Look for complete sample reference sheets at the end of this chapter.*)

What Should I Say?

In today's job market, it's acceptable and even recommended that you coach your references on what to say about you if they are contacted by your prospective employer. Again, make sure that they have a copy of your resume. In addition, it's a good idea to give them some sample job postings and cover letters to show them what kinds of positions you are pursuing. An added bonus: They may give you valuable feedback on your resume and cover letter that will help you improve those documents.

Discuss your strengths with each of your references, reminding them of your accomplishments when you worked together. Give them an understanding of how those accomplishments relate to the target job. This will help your references frame their answers in a way that advances your candidacy. Your goal is not to put words in their mouths, but to provide them with as much information as possible about your job search so that they can answer questions from employers in ways that will help you.

It's also vitally important that you and your references discuss the circumstances of your departures from earlier positions. You and each of your references should be in agreement about what they will say about how and why you left the job where they worked with you. As you'll see when you read the tips at the end of this chapter, you can avoid some embarrassing moments that can destroy your job search by addressing these issues up front. Sometimes this results in a decision not to use a particular person as a reference, but better to know that before you provide their name to a potential employer and have your candidacy inadvertently derailed.

After an interview, it might be beneficial to contact your references and let them know that you just had an interview for a position at Company X, and reiterate to them the key points you feel are relevant.

Secondary References

More and more frequently, recruiters and employers are seeking secondary references. The way this works is that the prospective employer will call one of your references and, near the end of the conversation, ask, "So, is there anyone else you know whom I can talk to about this candidate?" If your reference is unprepared, he or she may blurt out the name of someone who is not among your coached references— and possibly someone whom you'd prefer not be contacted to discuss your capabilities.

The solution to this is simple: Gather a list of six to eight references. When you're asked to supply references to a prospective employer, give them only three from your list. The three you choose can vary from situation to situation, depending on the employer's needs and the position you're applying for. Meanwhile, be sure to coach all of the people on your list to talk about your accomplishments and your value to an employer. Give each of your references a copy of the complete list, and explain to them that if, during the course of providing a reference, they are ever asked for a secondary reference or references, they should provide another name from the list you prepared. This approach closes the loop and ensures that the prospective employer will be talking only with coached references who are already expecting a call.

Tips From the Pros

Mary Ann had just completed her third round of interviews for an exciting new position. The interviews had all gone quite well, and she was asked to submit references for the prospective employer to contact. Unfortunately, Mary Ann never contacted any of her references to fill them in on her career plans and recent accomplishments. The result: her references were caught off guard and were less than stellar. Always request permission to use a person's name as a reference and provide them with a copy of your updated resume. Coach your references by telling them about the position's responsibilities and requirements the employer is seeking. On your reference document, include the name, contact information, relationship to you, and a statement about the type of skills/experience they would be able to discuss about you.

Louise Garver, CPRW, MCDP, CMP, JCTC, CLBF, CPBS, CEIP, COIS

Career Directions LLC

Your references, resume documents, and interview performance need to work together in order [for you] to receive job offers. Reference contacts are used to help you in your job search. Helping them know what to say will improve their effectiveness. Maintain communication with your references, keep them up-to-date on your job search, and let them know when they may be contacted. Remind them of your successes, achievements, value to the company, and your favorable interaction with co-workers and employers. A "cheat sheet" can be given to contacts listing specific skills and experiences that you would prefer them to mention. This works well in letting references know what you want to be passed to potential employers.

Kris Plantrich, CPRW, CEIP

ResumeWonders Writing and Career Coaching Services

Reference checking is one of the final stages in the recruitment process. References, if properly prepared, can convince and confirm that employers can feel confident in their intention to make a job offer. Call each individual to advise them that you have attended an interview and thank them for allowing you to provide their name as one of your references. Send each reference a list of your top five skills and talents as they relate to the role.

Tanya Taylor, CHRP, CRS

TNT Human Resources Management

The worst thing you can do as a job seeker is to allow an experienced Human Resources Manager to contact your unprepared references and begin to grill them about you. Yet many job seekers do not make sure their references are prepared and primed to talk to your future employer. Does your reference have a copy of your current resume? They must! Can you say your boss really knows ALL of the things you get done around the office? Most don't—so give them a cheat sheet. Your work is not done when you get the new job. Be sure to go back and thank your references profusely. Thank-you notes are important. Also, be sure to stay in touch with your references...you may need them again someday. Holiday cards and birthday cards are a great way to stay in touch.

Gail Frank, NCRW, CPRW, JCTC, CEIP, MA

Employment University

If you are changing careers, it is vital to make your references understand what kind of position you are pursuing. Coach them so they understand why you are pursuing that position and how your skills transfer to new roles. For example, if you are a nurse who is seeking a career in pharmaceutical sales, your references need to talk about your ability to get along well with doctors, your strong presentation skills, and your ability to build relationships. Send your references a copy of your new resume, and use it to help them see how you are re-branding yourself. Tell a story or two that will help your references see you in this new role. Ask them if they have any questions about how to present you.

Clay Cerny

AAA Targeted Writing & Coaching

Make sure you talk with your selected references about your "exit statement." The exit statement is what you tell prospective employers when asked "Why did you leave your last job?" It is critical that each of your references echo your reply; if not, they could really hurt your chances of securing an offer. Here's an example of how things can go awry: Judy had several interviews, which she thought went well, yet she was not receiving offers. Her last job ended for what she described as "a departmental reorganization that led to the elimination of her position." When I phoned her references and indicated that I was checking employment references for "Judy Smith," I was startled when her last employer responded with this statement: "It was quite obvious to all of us that Judy's main interest in working here was to find a husband. I spoke to her about her inappropriate comments and flirting with male coworkers, and when it did not end, we had to let her go." Judy could have taken legal action, but the more pragmatic approach was to remove this individual from her reference list and focus her time and energy on things that would help her more quickly transition to a new career.

Norine Dagliano, NCRW, CPRW, CFRW/CC

ekm Inspirations

You want your references to honestly answer any questions that may be asked of them about your overall job performance. Line up people to serve as references that you can trust to be honest about your job performance. Help a reference anticipate the type of tough questions they could be asked. Warn references to expect questions about your ability to handle work-related stress. Be sure your reference knows why you left a previous employer and how to positively describe any difficult circumstances surrounding your departure. Furnish a list of achievements you've demonstrated while working with them and provide examples of your relevant job skills.

Doris Appelbaum, BA, MS

Appelbaum's Resume Professionals, Inc.

You wouldn't ask someone to help you sell your house, and not provide them with a fact sheet about the house, its key selling features, and what sets it apart from the competition. In the same light, don't ask someone to help sell you to an employer without giving them an up-to-date fact sheet, discussing your key selling features, and telling them why you outshine the competition. If one of your references does not agree with how you are marketing yourself, then it would be a good idea to exclude him or her from your reference list.

Norine Dagliano, NCRW, CPRW, CFRW/CC

ekm Inspirations

KARL GREGORY
27 Pine Forest Cove
Syracuse, New York 13217
555-555-5555
karlg@resumesos.com

PROFESSIONAL REFERENCES:

Mr. Paul Vincent
President & CEO
St. Joseph's Health Care Corporation
123 Genesee Boulevard
Syracuse, New York 13250
(555) 555-5555
Former Superior

Ms. Ann Marie Kelly
Executive Administrative Assistant
St. Joseph's Health Care Corporation
123 Genesee Boulevard
Syracuse, New York 13250
(555) 555-5555
(555) 555-5555 (FAX)
Former Direct Report

Ms. Lois Marion
Former Director of Business Services
St. Joseph's Health Care Corporation
14 High Plains Village
Laredo, Texas 75123
(555) 555-5555
Former Colleague

Mr. Buford Raymond
Former Director of Protective Services
St. Joseph's Health Care Corporation
20 Baldwin Bend
Walworth, New York 14579
(555) 555-5555
Former Colleague

Serena L. Montgomery

732 Lafayette Circle ♦ Ithaca, New York 14850 ♦ 555.555.5555 ♦ E-mail: SMontgomery@ResumeSOS.com

Personal and Professional References

Rebecca J. Travanti
President, Advisory Board
American Red Cross of the Panorama Valley
555.555.5555
Becky@aol.com
(Former Supervisor)

Jared VandenBruhl
Manager, Retired
ExtraOrdinary Financial Services
555.555.5555
JVB@cs.com
(Former Employer)

Alexander H. Patrick
IT Consultant
(Former Owner, Laptop Systems)
555.555.5555
AHPatrick@buffalo.rr.com
(Former Employer)

Chapter 4

▶ Simple Truths About Wardrobe and Grooming for Your Job Interview

It's an old adage that you never get a second chance to make a first impression. Ironically, your job search will likely provide you with several opportunities to make a first impression. Your resume and cover letter make a first impression about your qualifications, which, hopefully, will lead an employer to contact you. When the employer calls to arrange a face-to-face interview or conduct a screening interview on the phone, you have the opportunity to make a second first impression based on how you handle yourself on the phone. Finally, when you show up for a face-to-face interview, you make perhaps the most important first impression of the job-search process—how you look.

The simple truth is that appearance matters in a wide array of social and business settings. Whether that's fair is a discussion for another time and place, but the practical, pragmatic, no-nonsense truth is that your appearance establishes an impression in the eye of the beholder that can be difficult to change, especially if it's a negative one. Image consultants will tell you that more than half of another person's perception of you will be based on how you look. According to one colleague who works with high school students entering the workforce for the first time, several employers have told her, "I don't care about the resume. I'll hire the best-dressed kid who walks through the door."

Most of us (this author included) aren't blessed with movie-star good looks; this simply means that we have to pay that much more attention to "packaging"—our wardrobe and grooming. Careful attention to the clothes we wear, how we wear our hair, and our body language can produce an image that is favorably received by hiring managers and potential coworkers. In this chapter, we will discuss how best to prepare yourself to make that best possible first impression.

Tips From the Pros

A job interview is your opportunity to win a job offer. It's also your opportunity to learn things that will factor into your decision about whether you want to work at the company in question. So why not do everything you can to get an offer? You can always decline if you decide it's not a good fit. Don't show up in clothing that makes a strong personal or political statement, thus giving the interviewer an easy reason to exclude you. Make a strong, positive impression with your wardrobe and grooming choices. Get the offer and then decide. It's up to you.

Gail Smith Boldt

Arnold-Smith Associates

First impressions are lasting features for most people, and that includes interviewers who are trained to observe their applicants. Arrive at least 10 minutes early with clean, pressed clothing of a somewhat conservative or business fashion. Remember that the interviewer(s) will make written and mental notes of your overall appearance and attire when evaluating your interview.

Edward Turilli

AccuWriter Resume Services

Understand the Corporate Culture

In Chapter 2, we talked about researching the company to better understand what the employer's needs are and how your unique skill set addresses those needs. Part of that research process should also include how people dress and behave in that environment. Some companies are very conservative: In my hometown, there's a billion-dollar company employing thousands of people nationwide, that has a very strict wardrobe and grooming policy which dictates that women wear skirts or dresses, and men wear dress shirts and ties. It even prohibits facial hair and body piercings. This may seem restrictive by 21st-century standards, but the policy exists nonetheless. People interested in working for this employer must conform to the code if they wish to get past an initial interview. On the other hand, there are technology companies on both coasts that encourage individuality, where even senior management can rarely be found in business suits. Most employers fall somewhere in between these two extremes, but whatever the accepted norm for a particular business, it's important for you as the candidate to understand the culture and do your best to emulate it when preparing for your interview.

Some candidates will stand outside the building or sit in the employee parking area to observe how people entering and leaving are dressed. When scheduling an interview, it's also reasonable to ask what the dress policy is. This information might even appear somewhere on the firm's Website, especially if it's a large organization. Of course, if you know friends who work at the target company, they can be your best source for intelligence about dress codes and company culture.

Regardless of what you have learned about the company culture, a general rule of thumb is to dress for the interview at a level one step above the position you're applying for. That usually means dressing as you would expect your prospective supervisor to dress. Generally speaking, if the job opening is for an office position, a business suit for men and a pant suit or conservative skirt or dress with tasteful accessories for women will serve you well. If you're applying for a blue collar position or one in which you'll be performing physical activities, more casual (but clean and neat) wardrobe choices may be appropriate—for men, perhaps khaki trousers and a collared sport shirt, but not jeans and a T-shirt. The key is to project an image that says you respect yourself enough to put your best foot forward and that you would represent the company well, even if your job is an internal one without direct customer contact.

Tips From the Pros

It is important to find out the dress code and preferences of a company before going for an interview. Many times Websites will provide a specific dress code for the entire corporation. If it's not on the Website, find someone who works there or call the company and ask. It would be very unfortunate if your appearance lost you the chance at a terrific job.

Kris Plantrich, CPRW, CEIP
ResumeWonders Writing & Career Coaching Services

Remember, while you may not need to dress up daily once you get in the job, going to the interview looking "put together" is very important. The thing to remember about an interview is that your attire tells the employer that you take them and their work environment seriously. It's not about your needs; it's about the employer's needs. By understanding this, you are increasing your chances of getting the job.

Dawn L. Rasmussen, CTP, CMP
Pathfinder Writing and Career Services, LLC

General Tips About Personal Grooming

You should be mindful of your breath when preparing for job interviews. Bad breath can be a real show stopper. If you have the opportunity, you should brush your teeth and rinse with mouthwash just prior to leaving for the interview to give yourself the freshest breath possible. Of course, that's not always practical unless the interview is first thing in the morning. Be sure to have breath mints or a breath-freshening gum or spray available, and use them as close to the time of the interview as possible. However, when you walk into the interview you shouldn't have anything in your mouth, so make sure you finish your mints or discard your gum before the interviewer greets you.

Along these lines, be mindful of any foods or beverages you consume prior to the interview, and what kind of aroma they leave on your breath or on your clothing. It's best to avoid onions, garlic, or other heavy spices; even coffee or milk will affect your breath, so be ready with the breath mints or gum. Tobacco also will leave a smell on your breath and your clothing that can be difficult to mask. If you're a smoker, you may feel as though you need that last cigarette before you go into the interview, but if you can avoid smoking right before the interview, especially in a confined space (such as your car), it will be to your advantage.

You should also be careful with perfume, cologne, lotion, or aftershave. What may seem like a perfectly delightful aroma to you may be offensive to others or, worse yet, might elicit an allergic reaction in some. Even if neither of these circumstances applies, too much fragrance can be overpowering and therefore distracting and objectionable. For women, a tried and true trick is to spray a fragrance into the air and walk through it to capture a subtle scent without it being overpowering. For men, a drop or two (no more) on the end of a finger and then rubbed onto the skin will typically be sufficient.

Tips From the Pros

Plan for wardrobe emergencies by always having these essentials at the ready:

- Safety pins, transparent tape, or a mini stapler for torn pant hemlines.
- A stain remover pen such as "Tide to Go" or another popular brand.
- White towel and a bottle of water for removing soil from shoes.
- Mini sewing kit for popped buttons.
- Grooming essentials (mints, comb, tissues, lip balm).

Tamara Dowling, CPRW
SeekingSuccess.com

Wardrobe and Grooming Tips for Women

The diversity of choices available in women's fashion presents business wardrobe challenges for women that their male colleagues don't face. Generally speaking, when planning for a job interview, you should lean toward conservative choices, with everything in moderation. Be careful not to overdo it with your makeup or jewelry, and be sure that your shoes are shined and in good repair. Two-piece suits or a jacket with a coordinating skirt or trousers are recommended (solid colors such as blue, gray, and black are best). Complement these with a solid colored blouse that coordinates with the rest of the outfit. An appropriate dress with a matching or coordinating jacket is another good choice. For less conservative business environments, adding a bit of color with a print blouse or scarf may be appropriate. A client I know who has interviewed for several senior leadership roles is fond of her red "power suit" for situations in which she wants to make a statement. Along these lines, be sure to consider how various colors complement your skin tone and reflect your personality.

Modesty is the byword. Avoid see-through blouses, bare midriffs, or skirts that rise more than a couple of inches above the knee when you're seated. Be sure to wear clothes that fit you well. Also, choose fabrics that wear well; for example, if you have a fairly long car ride, linen fabrics may become excessively wrinkled by the time you reach the interview. If you're traveling some distance, an option is to allow yourself time to stop somewhere and change into your interview outfit once you're close to your destination.

Make sure your shoes are shined and the heels are in good repair. Closed-toe pumps or flats are generally the best choices; be sure to avoid extremely high heels or boots. The color of your shoes should coordinate with the rest of your outfit. Hosiery should be neutral in color, without pattern or overt texture.

If you wear jewelry, it should accent your appearance and not be a distraction. Large hoop earrings, multiple bracelets on each arm, too many rings, and ostentatious necklaces all divert attention from your face, which is where the interviewer's attention should be focused. The "jingle-jangle" of large earrings or charm bracelets will also distract from your answers to the interviewer's questions. A good rule to follow is one ring per hand, one bracelet per wrist, and one earring per ear. Visible body piercings other than earrings are also not recommended.

Your hair should be clean and neatly styled off your face. Try to stay away from styles that require the excessive use of hair products such as mousse or hairspray. If you color your hair, make sure the roots are colored, as well. Long hair can be pulled back in a neat ponytail or put up—again, with the goal of keeping it out of your face and achieving an overall neat appearance. If you wear makeup, it should be applied sparingly to provide a natural appearance; bright hues should be avoided. Use makeup and powder to camouflage any visible tattoos. Nails should be clean and neat, and polish, if any, should be clear or neutral in color. If you have difficulty typing or dialing the phone, your nails are probably too long and should be trimmed.

Tips From the Pros

Your goal during the interview is to be remembered for what you said, not what you were wearing. Strive for [a] well-groomed hairstyle that is off the face; avoid excessive or distracting jewelry such as multiple bangle bracelets; stick to one pair of earrings; remove nose rings, eyebrow rings, etc.; no chewing gum during the interview. Choose your outfit the night before the interview to avoid rushing to put an outfit together too close to the time of the interview.

Barbara Safani

Career Solvers

First impressions may have a strong effect on the rest of the interview, since many people form quick, initial opinions. Your grooming, posture, and clothing will help the interviewer view you as an appropriate potential employee. Don't let your appearance create a roadblock to obtaining the job. Wear clothes you have worn before, including shoes. The last thing you want is to be uncomfortable. Likewise, check that your interview outfit still fits well. Avoid extremes, fads, frilly clothes, overly bold or busy patterns, severely tailored suits, loud colors, or poor color combinations. Think banker. It may seem boring; however, you want to be remembered for your qualifications and not your looks. Make sure your nails are clean and filed and remember to clean your eyeglasses.

Freddie Cheek

Cheek & Associates, LLC

Each company has its culture. When you schedule the interview, ask what would be appropriate or call the human resources department and ask what the company's dress code is. Some people go to the place where they will be interviewing and stand outside to check out employees' clothes. Wear something somewhat dressier than the employees wear to work. Never wear jeans or T-shirts. Jackets are always safe for women, with slacks or a skirt. They pull outfits together and can cover many figure problems. But the suit is still a staple in some professions. Make sure the garment fits properly and is of the best quality you can afford. Pant suits are still somewhat controversial. Some say women should always wear a skirt. But rules are changing. Hillary Clinton wears her now-trademark pant suit with little serious criticism for it.

Doris Appelbaum, BA, MS

Appelbaum's Resume Professionals, Inc.

Stacey was interviewing for an animal caretaker position in the education center at the local Zoo. She dressed for her interview in a frilly blouse—short, black skirt—stockings and heels—her long blond hair flowing over her shoulders. She looked fabulous, but it was all wrong! She looked like a cocktail waitress, not like someone who would be comfortable handling snakes, bottle-feeding baby bears, or cleaning up after messy raccoons. After some coaching, she returned wearing Dockers and casual shoes, a shirt with a button-down collar and a vest, and her hair pulled back in a ponytail. Still demonstrating that she cared about her appearance; but, this time she made the right impression for the targeted position. Interviewing is a lot like auditioning for a play. To get the part, you must look the part. The right shoes, clothes, hair, and makeup can get you a starring role!

Norine Dagliano, NCRW, CPRW, CFRW/CC

ekm Inspirations

Wardrobe and Grooming Tips for Men

Men have a much easier time of it than their female colleagues when it comes to wardrobe choices. The tried-and-true blue suit, with a light blue shirt and red tie, will still get you in the door. However, there are other choices to consider, and a number of details to keep in mind that will set you apart from the crowd.

Let's face it guys—very few of us have a keen sense of color when it comes to wardrobe. If you're among the majority that falls into that category, don't be shy about seeking some help, whether it's from your significant other or the salesperson at your favorite men's store. Whomever you choose to ask for help can assist you in developing a couple of surefire ensembles for you to wear to job interviews that will allow you to make a favorable impression. On the other hand, if you're stuck on your own, there are a few key things to remember.

Again, it's hard to go wrong with a dark blue suit; a charcoal gray suit is an excellent second choice. Personally, my hair color and skin tone go well with brown, so I always have a brown suit available. That's where a friend with an eye for color can be helpful in deciding what looks good and what to avoid. In a more casual setting, a blue blazer with gray trousers or a sport coat with coordinating trousers can be appropriate.

White shirts are the "old reliable," but in this day and age, a range of acceptable colors is available. With very few exceptions, your shirt should be a solid color and should coordinate with your suit. You should always wear a long-sleeved shirt with a suit or sport coat, even in summer, and be sure that the collar and cuffs are in good condition (not frayed or stained from perspiration). The shirt should be ironed, perhaps with light starch in the collar and cuffs. If you're not up to the task and have no one to help, most dry cleaners and laundry services will launder and press dress shirts for a modest fee.

Choose a tie that coordinates with your outfit. This is where your wardrobe consultant will be worth his or her salt. For example, all shades of blue don't automatically look good together and someone with a sharp eye for such things can be invaluable in detecting the subtle differences. Themed ties featuring animals or the logo of your favorite football team are a no-no. On the other hand, there are many geometric and floral prints that will complement your shirt and suit without appearing "unmasculine." A solid or traditional diagonally striped tie are reliable standbys if that's more to your taste. When tied (preferably with a symmetrical Windsor knot), the tip of the tie should just touch your belt buckle.

Your socks should be dark—preferably black, or at least a close match for the color of your trousers. Shoes should be lace-up dress shoes (no athletic shoes), and they should be well shined, with heels and soles in good repair. Choose either black or brown shoes, depending on what will coordinate with the rest of your outfit.

Jewelry for men should be very conservative. A nice watch, your wedding ring if you wear one, and/or a class ring from high school or college are all appropriate. Avoid chains and bracelets, and do not wear any earrings to the interview—not even that single diamond stud. Likewise, jewelry in other body piercings should be removed.

Your hair should be neatly trimmed and your neck cleanly shaved. If you are losing your hair, avoid the "comb-over" and seriously consider a shorter style. Believe it or not, this will take emphasis off the fact that you have a bald spot. (And by the way, shorter hair is currently in fashion; I made this choice recently and have been pleased with my new look—as is my wife!) If you wear a beard and mustache, they should be neatly and evenly trimmed. Depending on the culture of the company you are targeting, you may decide, at least temporarily, to shave the beard and mustache to conform to the norm of the prospective employer.

Tips From the Pros

Tie, shirt, and socks ought to be subdued in style and color (avoid Mickey Mouse and horse ties unless applying at Disney World or Churchill Downs). Suits are usually the best and safest choice, but a blue or brown sport coat with matching or color-coordinated trousers is acceptable. Shun string ties and large belt buckles. Play it safe and hide tattoos or facial piercings whenever possible.

Edward Turilli
AccuWriter Resume Services

Make sure your interview outfit looks "put together." Your suit, shirt, and tie should all work with each other to enhance your overall appearance. If you lack a sense of color and style, consult someone who can help. Even the discount men's stores at the mall typically have someone on staff who understands how to build a complete ensemble around a basic blue or gray suit. You don't have to buy everything they recommend, but you can get good ideas on how to put together a look. Friends, family, or store personnel often take great pleasure in helping candidates look sharp for that big interview.

Gail Smith Boldt
Arnold-Smith Associates

If you have a long drive to the interview, keep your suit jacket on a hanger and wait until you arrive at the interview site to put it on. This will prevent wrinkles and help to keep the suit looking fresh (instead of like you slept in it). This applies to sitting on an airplane, as well. If at all possible, try to hang the jacket on a hanger, or lay it neatly folded in the overhead to minimize wrinkles. If you're traveling out of town to an interview and arrive the night before, just before turning in for the night hang your interview clothes in your hotel room bathroom. Fill the tub with the hottest water you can get from the tap, and close the door. This will usually steam most of the wrinkles out of a suit and dress shirt without having to iron them.

Gail Smith Boldt
Arnold-Smith Associates

Body Language

We've already discussed how you have a number of opportunities to make a first impression on interviewers. Your body language is yet another example of this. Body language can start even before you meet the interviewer, and continues right through to the moment you drive away after the interview. Be prepared to greet the interviewer with a hearty handshake and engaging smile to set the tone, maintain an appropriate level of eye contact throughout the interview, and sit upright and poised in a way that shows attentive enthusiasm without appearing nervous. At the end of the interview, shake hands in parting and maintain your "stage presence" as you leave. Remember, someone may be observing you all the way to your car and as you drive away.

One colleague who coaches job seekers on body language spends 15 or 20 minutes teaching participants how to shake hands. Something so common and fundamental seems so simple, but it's yet another first-impression opportunity that is easily mishandled. You should reach for the other person's hand so that your hand meets his or hers midway between the two of you. The webbing between your thumb and index finger should meet the same webbing on the other person's hand, and your fingers should wrap around the heel of his or her hand with the tips of your fingers touching his or her wrist. Grip the hand firmly, but don't squeeze too hard—you want to grip the hand, not crush it. Gently pump no more than three or four times and release. Simultaneously, you should make eye contact, smile, and greet the person with "pleased to meet you, I'm so-and-so" or a similar appropriate phrase. That sounds like a great deal to think about, and it is. Practice it with a friend a few times until it feels natural and effortless.

Avoid the "dead fish" or "limp dishrag" handshake, in which you hang your hand out there and essentially make the other party do all the work. And again, don't crush the other person's hand with the grip of death just to prove how strong you are. Women should shake hands confidently and assertively. Don't forget about eye contact: Looking down or off to the side gives the other party the impression you lack confidence or are shifty.

As you walk to the interview room, keep your head up, shoulders back, and maintain a stride that keeps pace with the interviewer. Allow him or her to lead the way, or, if space permits, walk next to the interviewer, turning your head to listen to what he or she is saying as you walk along. As you enter the interview room, allow your interviewer to motion to where you should sit and let that person take his or her seat.

You should have both feet flat on the floor at all times (no crossing your legs or hooking your foot around a chair leg), and sit a little bit forward in the chair with your back straight. Place your briefcase or any other materials you brought with you on the floor next to the chair, not on the desk or table. If you brought a notebook or legal pad (an absolute must!), it is acceptable to have that on your lap along with a copy of your resume.

During the interview, you should listen attentively to the interviewer, making eye contact but not boring a hole in his or her forehead with your stare. Nod when it seems appropriate to show interest and to demonstrate that you are paying attention. It's perfectly acceptable to look down to take notes on your legal pad and glance at other spots on the room from time to time—just be careful not to appear uninterested in what the interviewer is saying.

When it's your turn to speak, once again, eye contact is important. Be careful not to speak too quickly, which is easy to do when you're feeling nervous. It's okay to pause for a few seconds before answering a question. This demonstrates that you are thoughtful and gives you a chance to gather your thoughts. Use hand gestures sparingly so that they don't become a distraction.

If you brought a professional portfolio with you, place it on the desk or table in front of you when invited to do so. Turn it around so that the interviewer can read the pages and view any graphics while you talk about them. Again, take your time and don't speak too quickly. You want the interviewer to have a chance to soak in the information in front of him or her. Depending on the circumstances, you may offer to leave the portfolio with the interviewer at the end of your presentation.

When the interview is over, you should wait for the interviewer to stand up first. If your interviewer offers to walk you out, withhold the farewell handshake until you part in the lobby. If the interviewer chooses to remain in the office, be sure to shake hands before leaving. Demonstrate the same level of enthusiasm and energy you displayed during your initial greeting. If you have the opportunity to do so, it's always a nice touch to thank the receptionist and wish him or her a pleasant day as you're leaving. You never know what part he or she may play in the decision-making process. In fact, keep in mind when you arrive that this person is watching you and may report his or her observations to the interviewer after you leave.

Briskly walk to your car, get in, and drive away. Save that cell phone call to your sweetheart or that must-have cigarette until you're safely away from the parking lot, perhaps for when you stop at the shopping mall or convenience store just down the street. Someone may be watching out the window to see how you behave when you think you're not being observed. In the same vein, try to wash the car and clean out the back seat before going on your interview. Occasionally, an interviewer will walk you all the way to your car just to see what you drive and how well it is maintained.

Tips From the Pros

Maintaining eye contact with the interviewer shows you are a good listener. Looking down at the floor or around the room rather than at the interviewer could be interpreted as not being completely truthful or [as] a desire to be somewhere else. However, at the other extreme, staring directly into the interviewer's eyes would make him quite uncomfortable. A constant gaze could send a message of aggression or at the very least, a sign of social awkwardness, leading to an inaccurate judgment about you. In face-to-face conversations, the most natural approach is occasionally looking away for a few seconds then returning your eyes to the speaker. If the interviewer gesticulates to make a point, glance briefly at the hand gestures, but always return to the face. For you male candidates, if you are being interviewed by an attractive female, don't think she doesn't notice when you cast your eyes below her neck. Whether it's inadvertent or intentional, you can almost bet that she will take note of this sexist mannerism in her assessment of you.

Melanie Noonan

Peripheral Pro, LLC

During interviews, your body language should convey confidence and sociability through direct eye contact, firm hand-shakes, pleasant disposition and smile, and clear and articulated words. Even your walk should be straight and strong with your head held high. Others will take this to mean you are confident in your skills and experience and in your ability to succeed at the job. A genuine smile and friendly demeanor demonstrate your potential to work well with others in the department and be the right fit for the job. Be aware of other non-verbal cues, such as facial movement, shaking a leg, foot or your hands excessively, and even a laugh, any of which can work against you. Videotaping yourself in mock interviews is a great tool for understanding how others see you and your actions.

Kris Plantrich, CPRW, CEIP

ResumeWonders Writing and Career Coaching Services

Body language may not start with the interview. It can begin the moment the interviewer sees you, and this can be outside the interview room in, for example, the reception area. Once, at an interview with a very senior company manager—penthouse suite scenario—I introduced myself to the receptionist, sat down in a very soft leather chair, and became engrossed in a magazine. Suddenly, the interviewer came bounding out of his office—hand extended. I was caught by surprise and shook hands with him while I was still struggling to get up. Effectively, he was dominating me and I was subservient—not a promising start to an interview. So, wait standing up and alert. If the interviewer comes out to greet you, the eye contact will be at the same (neutral) level. And don't get engrossed in the magazines!

Brian Leeson MSc

Vector Consultants Pty Ltd

Your body language can say more than you think to an interviewer. Your goal at every step along the way is to convey the message that you are interested in the position and excited to be a part of the conversation at hand. Sit on the edge of your seat, slightly leaning forward toward the interviewer. The opposite stature, sitting all the way back in your seat, may be proper posture, but subtly, it may not convey the interest and intensity that you'd like the interviewer to perceive. You want your body language to match the tone of your voice and your word selection. With subtle changes, your body language can help convey the overall image that you are very excited about the opportunity. Employers often choose between two equally qualified candidates by who appears more enthusiastic about the position. Employers want to hire people who are excited about joining their company.

Laurie Berenson, CPRW

Sterling Career Concepts, LLC

Body language is not restricted to you. Your car can tell the prospective employer a lot about you. Suppose you've just returned from a family weekend and you have a job interview on Monday morning. Your car is a mess; the kids have smeared ice cream and who knows what else over the windows, and the dogs have licked it off, only making it worse. There are kids' toys scattered everywhere and the car is covered in dust from the dirt roads. To make matters worse, this vehicle is a bit down market from what you should be driving. You had a great interview and really impressed the interviewer, who was friendly and offered to walk you back to your car. In reality, the interviewer just wanted to look at your car. You may have just lost the job because of your car's body language. Options to prevent this from happening to you include:

- Clean the car—inside and outside.

- Park a few blocks away and walk. (Tell the interviewer you were early and found the walk refreshing.)

- Rent a nicer car for the day and tell the interviewer yours is in for servicing.

Brian Leeson MSc

Vector Consultants Pty Ltd

Chapter 5

▶ Simple Truths About
Getting to the Interview and
What to Take With You

Identifying your objective, setting your goal, and successfully navigating the twists and turns of your career path are all essential to achieving success. Hopefully by now you've researched the company, developed your success stories, lined up some killer references, and figured out what you should wear to your interview. Now it's time to think about the logistics of actually going to the interview. In this context, you literally need to know where you are going and how to get there. All of your planning could be for naught if you show up late or get lost because you were unsure of the route, or if you forget an important piece of information such as your reference sheet or professional portfolio. As with any successful endeavor, planning is key. This final phase of planning comes down to three important things: know where you're going and how long it will take to get there; remember what to take with you; and be prepared for the unexpected.

Location, Location, Location

When you schedule your interview, you should definitely ask for directions, even if you're pretty sure how to get there. If it's a large facility, be sure to ask which entrance you should use and where you should park. Don't assume that you'll be reporting to the main entrance or the human resources office; the interviewer may have something else in mind. Many company Websites have directions to their facilities; it's a good idea to go to the Website and print them out, even if you were given verbal instructions on the phone. You can also consult one of the online mapping tools. Mapquest is the most commonly known, but most of the major search engines have similar services that you can link to from their home pages. A word of caution:

There can be discrepancies and inaccuracies on these maps, and occasionally they won't give you the most efficient route from point A to point B. Of course, if you have one of the several onboard GPS navigation devices that have hit the market in recent years, you can also use that to plot your route. Whichever you choose to use, comparing a couple of sources is always a good practice.

For out-of-town trips especially, it can be very helpful to have a full map that shows a whole city or metropolitan area to give you perspective that you can't get from the small, detailed maps printed from online sources. If you do make a mistake and are off course, the larger city map may be your best hope of navigating back on course. If you belong to AAA, they will happily provide such maps and directions to their members, typically free of charge.

If your interview is local and you have any doubt about where you are going, make a dry run at least one day before. Drive the same route you plan on using to get to the interview and confirm the written directions. Also keep an eye out for road construction, one-way streets in locations where you didn't expect them, and other impasses. If it's possible to drive the route at the same time of day as when your interview is scheduled, you'll have the opportunity to observe traffic patterns and allow for anticipated delays. A drive that takes 20 minutes on a Sunday morning could easily take more than an hour during the Wednesday-morning rush hour. If the interview is out of town, you may still be able to do a dry run from your hotel to the interview site if you arrive the night before. In the alternative, get an extra early start to give yourself a "buffer" if you do indeed get lost or miss a turn. Regardless of where your interview is, plan to arrive 15 to 20 minutes before the appointment. In the best of circumstances, you'll have a few minutes to spend in the parking lot gathering your thoughts, and then in the restroom to take one last look in the mirror. In the worst of circumstances, it may allow you to still arrive on time.

Having What It Takes/Taking What You Need

There are a number of things you will want to take with you to an interview. On the one hand, you don't want to over-pack; on the other hand, you don't want to leave behind anything essential. For purposes of this discussion, there are really four scenarios you need to consider.

The local interview

For this interview, you leave your home or your current job, drive directly to the interview site, and return to home or work afterward. You're probably wearing your interview outfit when you leave, so the focus is on these key items: copies of your resume, your reference sheet, portfolio of accomplishments, copy of the job posting, directions to your destination, and other research materials you have accumulated.

If you're wearing a suit jacket, hang it in the back of the car and put it on just before you walk in for the interview.

The driving-out-of-town interview

This interview involves driving your own car or one you have rented. Be sure to include everything mentioned in the first scenario, but take advantage of the space you have in the car and take along other important things. Wear comfortable clothes to drive in and plan to change into your interview outfit some place close to the employer's location. If you're not sure about where to stop, there are many commercial truck stops on major highways that have facilities where you can change your clothes (or even take a shower, though hopefully you won't need one), or you can use the restroom in a fast-food restaurant. Of course, if you're staying overnight, you can change at your hotel. Take a complete second interview outfit and an extra set of "casual dress" clothes. This allows you the opportunity to recover from a wardrobe disaster, and also gives you options if you're invited to stick around for an after-hours activity. Hang your interview clothes on hangers in the back of your car, or lay them flat on the seat to avoid wrinkles. Make sure you have a fully stocked personal grooming kit and spare set of undergarments. If you take any prescription medications, include a two-day supply in your grooming kit, just to be safe.

The flying-out-of-town interview

This interview involves flying to another city and often staying overnight. This is perhaps the most challenging scenario. You'd like to be able to take everything you'd take if you were driving, but you need to travel light. The most efficient approach is to take a single carry-on bag. Be sure it meets airline size requirements, and be strategic about how you pack. (At this writing, the Transportation Safety Administration allows a single one-quart sealed plastic bag containing liquids in containers of 3 ounces or less; trial size or travel size toiletries will probably pass muster.) The biggest advantage is that you won't have to wait for luggage at your destination and you have little risk of losing anything along the way. In addition to resumes, portfolios, and reference sheets, include an extra shirt (or blouse) that matches your ensemble; your grooming kit including your medications; extra underwear; and something comfortable to wear on the flight home. If you're checking into a hotel before going to the interview, wear something comfortable on the plane and plan to change into your interview outfit. Packing it in your luggage may cause wrinkling, but your clothes will still be fresher than if you traveled in them. Hopefully you'll have the opportunity to use an iron to touch things up, or try the steamy bathroom trick mentioned in Chapter 4. Don't forget to take all the items mentioned previously in Scenario #1, and consider whether transporting your documents electronically, on a CD-ROM or a memory stick makes sense. You can then print them at the hotel's business center or a quick-copy store near the interview site. This could be more bother than it's worth, but it's one way to eliminate some bulk when you're packing.

The in-town interview

This interview involves using public transportation or walking. In this situation, a briefcase or tote bag that accommodates all of your papers is a good idea. It should be large enough to contain everything you plan to take along (pretty much everything that was mentioned in the first scenario). That way, you only have to worry about carrying one item. Depending on the weather, the reliability of buses or subways, and other logistical factors, consider taking a taxi to ensure you arrive on time and not disheveled by your journey. Make sure you have an umbrella and an appropriate overcoat, headgear, and footwear for the seasonal conditions you may encounter.

In Appendix A, you will find a comprehensive checklist of materials you should consider taking with you to your interview. Review that list, taking into consideration the recommendations offered previously, as well as the expert advice that follows:

Tips From the Pros

Arrive 10 to 15 minutes before your scheduled interview. Be certain you know the best travel route there, parking, and the time it takes to arrive well before your appointment. This will give you a chance to settle down, groom a final time, and familiarize yourself with the interview site.

Edward Turilli, M.A., CPRW

AccuWriter Resume Service

Obtain name, title, and pronunciation for all interviewers and put on an index card to bring along. Create [an] interview version of your resume (labeled as such) that has information for the job application not on the normal resume: past employers' full addresses and phone numbers, former supervisors' names, actual job start and end dates, and start and end salaries. Also, add full address, to and from dates, GPA, and number of courses (or quality points) for any degrees. Pack for the interview (briefcase or folder): extras resumes, references, pens, job posting, note pad, tissues, mints, erasers/Wite Out [correction fluid], application information, certificates of training, licenses, or certifications, and any other items you were asked to bring.

Freddie Cheek, M.S. Ed., CCM, CPRW, CWDP, CARW

Cheek & Associates, LLC

Prepare and have available a list of questions to ask or specific points you can check off as answered during the interview. If salary and benefit packages are going to be addressed, have the necessary documentation prepared as tools for negotiating. Finally and possibly the most important but often overlooked item, is your list of names, titles and area of work for those you will be in contact with and all those who will be sitting in on the interview.

Kris Plantrich, CPRW, CEIP

ResumeWonders Writing and Career Coaching Services

Creating a professional portfolio to take to an interview can set you apart from the competition. A portfolio offers concrete proof of the skills you will be discussing. And, if you typically get nervous, a portfolio gives you something to hold in your hands and takes the focus, at least temporarily, away from your face. A simple professional portfolio is a one-inch three-ring binder in a conservative color like black or navy, filled with plastic sheet protectors. Each sheet protector contains a document that shows an example of your skills. Start with your resume, your reference list, and letters of recommendation. After you have the basics, create a section specific to your field of work. For example, if you're a teacher, include your best lesson plans; if you're a bookkeeper, include sample QuickBooks pages; if you're a house painter, include photos of completed jobs. Use your portfolio as a tool throughout the interview. For example, if the interviewer asks you about your ability to write memos, you might show sample memos you have written for current or past employers.

Heather Carson, GCDF, CPRW, JCTC

Second Start

Part II

▶ Presentation

Chapter 6

▶ Simple Truths About
the Many Types of Job Interviews

In the never-ending struggle to identify and select the best possible candidates, employers have developed an increasingly diverse and complex array of interviewing styles and techniques. Each approach has its own benefits from the employer's perspective and each presents its own set of challenges for the job seeker. The key to success in facing any of these methods is to understand the interviewer's underlying agenda in using a particular type of interview: What information are interviewers attempting to elicit from you, the candidate? How can you use your knowledge of their motives to your advantage in forming your answers to their questions? These are the challenges that are addressed in this chapter.

How Do I Interview Thee?
Let Me Count the Ways

The table in Chapter 1 outlines 14 different types of interviews that you may encounter. On the next few pages, these various types of interviews will be discussed, giving you some insights into what to expect and how to cope with any of these scenarios. One interview type that is not explicitly mentioned is the "behavioral" interview. You will often see this term used in many of the currently popular interview books. It refers to an interview in which you are asked to describe how you would handle a particular situation that might arise in a work setting. Typically, it's in the format of "what would you do if…?" As you look at the types of interviews that follow, you will notice that many of them can and do incorporate the behavioral format, depending on the actual questions posed. Interviews over a meal and telephone interviews are given a more in-depth treatment than the others because of the special challenges they pose and their growing popularity.

The traditional

You're interviewed by the hiring decision-maker, who also happens to be the person who would be your direct supervisor. If this is for a technical position (in engineering or software development, for example), show up prepared to demonstrate your knowledge and expertise. This interviewer is likely someone who is at or above your level of technical proficiency and will ask you specific questions that probe your capabilities. Be prepared for any number of problem-solving scenarios.

The intermediary

You're interviewed by a representative of the HR department who may or may not be intimately familiar with the position for which you are applying (and may be screening for potential future interviews with the hiring authority). Although HR people may lack the technical knowledge that relates to the job, it's likely that they have discussed the opening with the hiring manager and have a list of criteria that you must meet. Presumably your resume was comprehensive enough to get you the interview, but be prepared to back up any credentials or educational claims you've made.

Tasks and challenges

You're presented with a specific task, such as prioritizing numerous items in an in-basket or solving a series of puzzles, and are evaluated on your judgment, creativity, and efficiency in completing it. This type of interview could easily be incorporated into a "traditional" or "intermediary" interview, or presented as an interview in its own right. It's fair to ask up front if there are any company policies or guidelines that you should be following so that you know what the rules are. When in doubt, use common sense: If you had to make a decision on your own, what does your gut tell you is the right thing to do?

Meet and greet

You spend an entire day meeting individually or in small groups with various key stakeholders. This process (ordeal?) often includes meals and facility tours. The employer wants to elicit a number of opinions about you from different perspectives within the organization. Your secret to success is to be consistent in your answers with everyone you encounter, and to do your very best to maintain your energy level throughout the day. Part of the test is to see if you have the stamina to make it through without appearing exhausted or showing frustration with the process.

Firing line

You're interviewed and evaluated by each member of a panel. This creates stress for you, which affords the interview panel the opportunity to see how you behave under pressure. While one interviewer is engaging you and asking a question, the others have the chance to observe your body language and look for any chinks in your armor. Try to remain calm, make eye contact with each "inquisitor," and don't be afraid to take control of the situation if you get bombarded by multiple questions. Make sure that you have names and contact information for each interviewer so that you can follow up appropriately.

Sink or swim

You're one of a variably sized group of candidates interviewed in the same space at the same time. Some interview coaches refer to this as a "cattle call," and it bears some resemblance to a Broadway audition in that respect. The interviewers are saving time by dealing with a group of applicants all at once. They're also looking for candidates who stand out from the crowd. Someone in the room is carefully watching to see who's paying attention and who's not, so be attentive to each speaker and wait your turn. If you've done your company research, you should be able to give insightful answers that will differentiate you from the masses. As with the panel, make sure you get everyone's name and contact information for follow up.

Groupthink

You're one of a small group of candidates asked to discuss an issue or solve a problem together, and are evaluated throughout the process. This is akin to an episode of *The Apprentice* in many ways. Your goal is to exhibit your capacity to work effectively in a team, but the scenario may also afford you the opportunity to demonstrate leadership skills by taking command of the situation. Be courteous and professional with the other members of the group, keeping in mind the qualities relevant to the targeted job opening and how you can effectively display them in this group dynamic.

Showtime

You're asked to prepare a presentation on a particular topic—for example, how you would overcome a challenge the organization currently faces—and deliver it to key stakeholders. Typically you will be given some advance notice of this performance. The employer may give you a topic or leave it up to you. If it's the latter, this is a golden opportunity to sell yourself as the solution to the company's problems. Use your presentation to offer the employer a strategic vision of what you would do during the first 30 or 60 days on the job. You can also demonstrate that you've researched the company's biggest challenges, and show that you are a strategic thinker by giving the interviewer(s) a viable plan that you can execute if they hire you.

Remote control

You're asked to go to a video conference site and are interviewed remotely by one or more people (the session will most likely be recorded). This saves the company the cost of flying you to their location. Be mindful of wardrobe choices. Stripes and plaids don't come across well on camera; solids are the safest way to go. A light blue or light beige shirt is better than a white one in this setting. Avoid any flashy jewelry that might cause a glare on camera. If you take presentation materials (and you should), make the print large enough to be seen (minimum 24-point type). Be sure to arrive early and gain a full understanding of how to use the equipment on your end.

Classic good cop/bad cop

Two interviewers question you, with one coming across as engaging and friendly while the other is cold and aggressive. Don't be fooled. Just as with the police interrogations you see played out on TV, both interviewers have the same motives. Their goal is to put you under stress and see if you react by giving them answers that reveal any weaknesses. As with a panel interview, maintain your cool. Take the questions one at a time and give well-reasoned, thoughtful answers to both interviewers, regardless of their attitude toward you.

Minute waltz

Similar to speed dating, you get 15 minutes with the interviewer to make an impression. This approach is currently popular for screening a large number of candidates for entry-level opportunities. If you have an elevator speech ready, this is the place to use it. You want to give succinct answers packed with information about how you can be a solution to an employer's challenges.

Problem solved

You're given a word problem to solve. Typically, it's not about math skills per se; it's about logic and the ability to work through a process to a solution. With apologies to Sherlock Holmes and Sir Arthur Conan Doyle, if you carefully consider the question and eliminate all the choices that are impossible, then what remains must (logically!) be the correct answer. Frequently, the answer is simpler than it seems at first glance, but the "obvious" answer may also be wrong. The secret to success is taking your time and carefully thinking the problem through to find a solution.

Let's do lunch

Just about everybody goes to lunch. You take your Aunt Maggie to celebrate her birthday, salesmen meet clients to close deals or thank customers for their business, and friends meet just to catch up. There's even a dating service that has a program called "It's Just Lunch" to connect busy young singles, giving them a (theoretically) low-pressure opportunity to get acquainted. What these scenarios have in common is the concept that meeting people over a meal creates a relaxed atmosphere in which people can converse, get acquainted, and enjoy each other's company. Where would the restaurant industry be without all of these people who go to lunch?

Having a job interview over lunch (or breakfast, or dinner) is a whole different ball game. Although the interviewer may want you to relax and let your hair down, it's important to be on your toes during mealtime interviews, because the opportunities for miscues and *faux pas* are even more numerous than in any of the other types of interviews we've discussed so far. The employer hopes you will relax and be yourself, and thus reveal an aspect of your character that might not otherwise have been apparent in a more structured setting.

Your goal should be to stay focused and composed, giving the interviewers a positive impression of you as a person and as someone who fits into their organization's culture. Most importantly, remember that it's still a job interview and that, as such, virtually every other bit of advice offered in this chapter and throughout the rest of the book still applies. Be sure to arrive on time and dress appropriately, prepare to answer all the tough questions, and be aware of your body language, including your handshake.

Etiquette

Hopefully you won't find yourself dining at an *haute cuisine* restaurant with a menu in a foreign language and lots of extra silverware and dishes. Should this happen, however, don't be intimidated; there's a good chance that others in your party aren't certain about which fork to use, either. There are a couple of very basic rules that will probably be sufficient for navigating such situations.

When it come to silverware, start from the outside and work in toward the dinner plate. As an example, the salad fork (which you will likely use first) is generally the outermost utensil to the left of the plate. If you follow this simple rule, you won't go too far wrong. If the seating arrangement is such that there are several place settings around a circular table, there may be some question as to which items are a part of your place setting and which belong to your neighbor. Generally speaking, your bread plate will be to the left, your coffee cup will be to the right, and your water glass will be somewhere close to your coffee cup. More specific details about such matters are easily found online at *www.cuisinenet.com*.

If the menu is in a foreign language, let the interviewer do the ordering, or ask the server to explain things to you. I went on an interview once in which the interviewer took me to a Chinese dim sum restaurant and delighted in demonstrating his knowledge of Chinese by doing all the ordering. (The food was superb, by the way.) Failing that, the wait staff is most likely accustomed to explaining to diners what each dish contains and how it's prepared.

Follow the interviewer's lead

As much as possible, allow your "host," the interviewer, to take the lead. Hopefully the server will recognize him or her as the head of your party and take his or her order first. You should follow suit by ordering something that's similarly priced. Likewise, wait to see if the interviewer orders dessert or an extra cup of coffee before ordering one yourself.

One way to hedge your bets and be prepared in case you get caught ordering first is to compliment the interviewer and ask him or her a leading question, such as, "This looks like a really nice place to have lunch. Do you come here often?" Depending on the answer, you can then follow up by asking what is really good there, if he or she has a favorite dish, and/or what he or she would recommend. Armed with that information, you should choose something that is around the same price and that will likely take about the same amount of time to prepare and eat. It's also generally a good idea not to order soup or salad with your entrée unless the host does so.

Things to remember

It's best to never order alcohol at a mealtime interview, regardless of what the interviewer does or invites you to do. There are several reasons why this is important, but two really stand out: First and foremost, alcohol, even one drink, can lower your inhibitions and cause you behave inappropriately, or cause you to reveal information that you'll later wish you hadn't. Remember what we said in the opening paragraph of this section: Remain focused and stay on your toes. Second, drinking alcohol at a business meeting—including a job interview— may be seriously frowned upon by the interviewer. Why risk it just to appear sociable?

Tips From The Pros

Interviews over lunch or dinner can be conducted anywhere from a fast-food restaurant to a first-class private dining club. A firm may choose a social setting for a meeting with a prospective employee, but however relaxed the atmosphere might be, the purpose of such a meeting is ultimately to conduct an interview. Prepare and remember to:

- Carefully plan your wardrobe.
- Practice a positive greeting.
- Avoid alcoholic beverages.
- Order food that is not messy to eat.

Loretta Heck
All Word Services

Being invited to a restaurant by your potential employer can mean that you are a finalist in the selection process. Your behavior in such a relaxed setting can make or break your chances. Make no mistake; you are under close scrutiny to assess your social graces in a non-work environment. Take your cue from your host and order a menu item in the same price range. Compliment your host on the choice of restaurant, even if you don't enjoy your meal. In casual conversations, be sure to take every opportunity to sell yourself. Describe instances when you demonstrated a skill related to the subject matter, and never let your guard down, especially during lighthearted moments. Try to refrain from drinking alcoholic beverages, as they may loosen your inhibitions, causing you to reveal inappropriate information that could be used to disqualify you. By the same token, note how your host treats the server. Think twice about accepting an employment offer from someone who exhibits a rude and demanding attitude. It could be an indication of how this manager will treat you once you are hired.

Melanie Noonan

Peripheral Pro, LLC

If ever you are asked to be interviewed over a meal, here is food for thought:

- Know the location of the restaurant, even if that means visiting the venue a day or two prior to your interview.

- Turn off your cell phone.

- Make sure you have thoroughly researched the company.

- Be polite to the restaurant staff.

- Do not order any alcoholic drink, even if invited to do so.

- Select a reasonably priced meal and order food that you can easily handle.

Daisy Wright, CDP BA

The Wright Career Solution

Can you hear me now?

As transportation costs continue to rise, more and more employers are conducting initial screening interviews by phone. In some cases, even second and third interviews may also take place over the phone. For the employer, this approach conserves resources by not having to pay travel expenses for candidates to fly or drive great distances to an interview and most likely stay at least one night in a hotel. In addition, there is a big time savings for employers. An HR representative can conduct phone interviews one after another without being required to walk to the lobby, escort the candidates back to the office, and lead the candidates back to the lobby at the conclusion of the interviews. Using the phone could easily save an interviewer 10 to 15 minutes per interview; if he or she is screening dozens of candidates for a position, that time adds up in a hurry.

Another possible reason for a phone interview is that the position in question calls for telephone skills. By talking to you on the phone, the interviewer can gain a sense of how you handle yourself on the phone and determine whether or not you would be the right fit for a customer service, technical support, or telemarketing position in which your primary interaction with customers is by phone.

Don't be put off by the fact that you're only being asked to interview by phone, and certainly don't fall into the trap of taking it all too lightly and thinking, *It's just a phone interview*. Recognize the pluses and minuses of the situation, prepare just as you would for a face-to-face interview, and capitalize on the subtle advantages that a phone interview will give you.

How phone interviews are different

The biggest difference between phone interviews and conventional interviews is, of course, that the interviewer and the candidate cannot see each other. This is the proverbial double-edged sword. On the one hand, your wardrobe and body language are of little significance and can't work against you; on the other hand, your hearty handshake and the portfolio of accomplishments you planned to take to your face-to-face interviews are of little help. However, with proper preparation, you can take advantage of these differences and deliver a winning performance during the interview.

Keep in mind that a phone interview is still an interview. Treat it with the same level of seriousness and commitment that you would if you were dressing in your best interview outfit and driving across town for a face-to-face meeting. Prepare a special place—in a den or study, if possible—where you can sit or stand (as some experts recommend) and conveniently refer to your resume and notes. If you slouch on the couch or relax in the chaise lounge by the pool, the interviewer will be able to tell. In addition, make sure your answering machine or voice mail has a professional sounding message, and coach family members on how to speak to callers who may be seeking to interview you for a new job. Be prepared for the unexpected call at an inopportune moment.

Using the differences to your advantage

The fact that the interviewer cannot see you gives you the opportunity to "cheat" a little bit in your interview preparation—or, at the very least, treat the interview as you would an open-book test. If you have an office or private space at home where you plan to conduct telephone interviews (this is highly recommended), prepare this space by posting a copy of your resume on the wall or in a spot where you can easily see it while you're on the phone. Likewise, arrange your research materials about the company in question so that they are easily referenced during the interview.

If you have an online portfolio or Web resume, you can use them to your advantage during a phone interview, as well. When it's your turn to talk about yourself and your accomplishments, ask the interviewer if Internet access is readily available. If it is, invite the interviewer to go to your site and browse it with you. As you talk about your accomplishments, you can direct the interviewer to the appropriate spot on the Website, which gives him or her a visual aid that reinforces what you're saying. In a face-to-face interview, this technique could be somewhat awkward and cumbersome in that it could detract from your interaction with the interviewer; during a phone interview, however, this technique makes perfect sense. It may even enhance the interaction by giving the interviewer something visual to focus on, as you are not in the same room together.

Select the right time and location

I've cautioned you several times to be just as well-prepared for a phone interview as for an in-person meeting. Along those lines, you want to have as much control of your environment and the timing as possible. If you are able to schedule the interview in advance, be sure to choose a time when you will be calm and collected. If you're a night owl, agreeing to be interviewed at 8 a.m. may not be a good strategy. If you know that the kids will be arriving home from school between 2:30 and 3:30 p.m., try to schedule the interview before 2 or after 4 p.m.

When you choose the time of the interview, hopefully you'll be able to be in your special space that you've prepared, with all of your reference materials, and where you won't be distracted or interrupted. Some interview coaches recommend dressing for the occasion, as well. If you're a "method actor" and need to look and feel the part to be able to perform, consider dressing in the business suit that you would have worn to a face-to-face meeting. Many experts also recommend standing up for the interview (something you can't usually do in person). Being on your feet naturally creates a level of alertness and just the slightest bit of tension that will, quite literally in this case, keep you on your toes.

Of course, you may find yourself getting ambushed by an interviewer calling without warning at a bad time and expecting to conduct the interview right then and there. The best approach is to politely ask the interviewer if you can either schedule a time later that same day or the following day, thus giving yourself time to prepare. If that doesn't seem possible and the interviewer is insistent on speaking with you right away, you certainly don't want to miss an opportunity. Ask the interviewer if he or she would mind holding for just a moment or two—or better yet, ask to call him or her back within the next five to 10 minutes. Whichever the interviewer agrees to, move quickly to your special interview place and gather your thoughts and your resources to be as prepared as you can be for the interview. In such circumstances, remaining calm and unflustered will demonstrate to the interviewer how you handle stressful situations and the unexpected. After all, that may well be why they called at such an inconvenient time in the first place.

Tips From the Pros

When there are many candidates for a job opening, employers will use telephone screening techniques to eliminate obviously unqualified applicants. Even though you expect prospective interviewers to call, you are at a disadvantage if you are caught off guard when it happens, and not given much of a chance to sell your worth to the company. Nevertheless, when you receive such a call, enthusiastically express your interest in the job, but don't hesitate to ask for a few minutes to get yourself ready and offer to call the person back. During this time, review your information about the company, the required functions of the job, and your competencies. Most likely the screener will use a standard checklist, asking all candidates the same questions that focus on technical skills but will also be probing for inconsistencies and personality traits that would fit the corporate culture. Your goal is to convince this screener that you meet or exceed the qualifications needed to be granted a full-fledged interview with the hiring manager.

Melanie Noonan
Peripheral Pro, LLC

When preparing for a phone interview, set up a "phone zone," preferably in a private, quiet room where you will have easy access to your resume, notes, paper, and a pen or pencil. In your phone zone, place a mirror in front of you, and practice the art of talking and smiling at the same time. Smiling while you talk will help you connect with the interviewer, as he or she will hear the smile in your voice. As the interviewer asks you questions, write down a couple of key words to guide your responses, keep them concise, and ensure you remember the original question. Also, practice your listening skills. Write the word "LISTEN" on a piece of paper and tape it in front of you as a gentle reminder. As you listen to the interviewer, try to identify what problems the company has that you could solve if hired. Then, use that information to position yourself as the candidate of choice by relating a story that showcases your success solving a similar problem for a previous employer.

Robyn Leigh Feldberg, CCMC, VAL
Abundant Success Career Services

Try to use a landline phone. Be sure there is no background noise. Turn off everything—cell phone, radio, fax machine, and speakers on your computer. Smile when you talk! Have a glass of water nearby, and warm up your voice. Listen carefully to the tone of the interviewer. Take note of how fast or slow they are speaking. Then, try to match their speaking style. If he/she talks fast and you talk slower, then pick up your speaking pace to match their pace. If they talk slow[ly] and you talk [quickly], then slow down a bit. Speak clearly into the phone. Put energy, enthusiasm, and body language into your voice!

Camille Carboneau Roberts, CFRW/C, CPRW, CEIP, CARW

CC Computer Services & Training

Take the phone call...sitting at [either] a table or desk and dress in either professional or business casual attire. Your voice and your choice of words are how you will convey yourself to the interviewer. Some people will be more comfortable sitting at a desk or table while others might prefer standing and the chance to walk around the room a bit as they answer. Either way, if you are conducting the telephone interview from home, avoid the temptation to conduct the interview lounging on the couch in a T-shirt and sweats. If you dress and "play" the part, your voice and intonation will benefit greatly. It's a subtle difference, but one that will work to your advantage.

Laurie Berenson, CPRW

Sterling Career Concepts, LLC

Close the interview in a way that will lead to a follow-up meeting. Show you're interested. When it feels right and it sounds like the interview is wrapping up, ask for a date to meet for face-to-face interview. For example: "This sounds like a great position and I know I could step in and contribute. I would love the opportunity to sit down with you in person and discuss this even further. When could we meet for an interview?" If the interviewer hedges or says "I'll call you," try to politely probe a little further. Ask, "When might I likely hear back from you?" If you are invited for the face-to-face interview, be certain to thank the interviewer and get the important details—when, where, with whom you are interviewing, the format of the interview or process (length and how many interviews are normally undertaken), and whether there is anything in particular you need to bring. Repeat the key details to make sure your notes are accurate. Be sure to thank the interviewer for the opportunity and his or her time. Do not hang up until the interviewer has hung up. Then, while everything is still fresh in your mind, make notes about what you were asked and how you answered. Be sure to write a short thank-you note to the interviewer.

Murray A. Mann and Rose Mary Bombela-Tobias

Global Diversity Solutions Group

If you receive an unexpected call from a recruiter and he or she expects to interview you right then and there, first, remain calm! Ask for some time to get yourself ready. For example: "Terrific...could you give me a moment to go to a room where we won't be interrupted?" or "Could you give me just a moment to close the door?" When they agree, cover the voice piece on the phone, and go to your quiet area where you have all of your job search material prepared, take two or three deep breaths, and then continue. If you are genuinely unable to devote enough time to an unscheduled phone interview or [aren't] ready to continue with the interview, politely ask the recruiter for an alternate time. It is preferable to proceed with the interview if it's possible that you might not get a call back. If you must reschedule then, offer to be the one who calls back at a scheduled time.

Murray A. Mann and Rose Mary Bombela-Tobias

Global Diversity Solutions Group

Do your research on the company/organization and the position. For example, read any local newspaper articles, journals, etc. that could give you insight into the position. Before the interview, write out the answers to the traditional and behavioral interview questions and lay them out in front of you along with your resume. Don't read your answers, but you can glance at them to help you remember what to say.

Marilyn A. Feldstein, M.P.A., JCTC, MBTI, PHR

Career Coach and Professional Speaker

A clear voice with enough inflection sounds more interesting. If you are nervous, try smiling while talking or taking a deep breath. Relax—think through the questions and make sure you answer them confidently and with concrete examples or numbers.

Kris Plantrich, CPRW, CEIP

ResumeWonders Writing and Career Coaching Services

Frequently there are pauses in an interview. Some interviewers use a long silent pause as a strategy to determine how a candidate handles stress. These pauses can be even more stressful during a phone interview because you cannot see the person's expressions. If you find yourself in a long pause, remain calm and use these simple tips. Avoid the urge to fill the void with chatter. Often candidates will assume the last answer given was not adequate, so they will share unnecessary additional information. If you completed your answer, stop and wait for the next question. Wait 10 seconds and then ask, "Have I answered your question?" Or you may ask, "Would you like another example?" Refrain from saying, "Are you still there?" You may use silence to your advantage. You can reflect on what you have said and plan additional points you want to make later in the interview. Periods of silence are a natural part of the ebb and flow; so don't be intimidated.

Tamara Dowling, CPRW

SeekingSuccess.com

A phone interview should be scheduled like any other interview. At the designated appointment time, make sure the dog is in the backyard and someone else is watching the kids. If a recruiter or hiring manager calls you without advance notice and wants to interview you on the spot, use caution. If the interview "conditions" are not optimal at the time of the call, it is best to tell the interviewer that you are very interested in the position, but need to schedule another time to have a conversation. That time can be as soon as 10 minutes later, [but] just make sure that you can take the call without being distracted. Have your notes in front of you. A phone interview is like an open-book test. You can have your company research and answers to potential interview questions right in front of you. Try putting key information on colored index cards and organize by category. Don't multitask. We have grown so accustomed to multitasking; however it can be counterproductive during a phone interview. Don't check your e-mail or stick a casserole in the oven while you are engaged in a phone interview. Act the same way you would for an in-office interview and maintain your focus.

Barbara Safani

Career Solvers

Chapter 7

▶ Simple Truths About
Routine Interview Questions

The title of this chapter is a bit of a misnomer because, in reality, there aren't any routine job interview questions. What we're really talking about in this chapter are the most routinely asked interview questions. These questions (I've picked 10 of the most common) are the ones that just about every interviewer asks, and if you've been on an interview recently, you've probably been asked several of them. The risk is that you may be lulled into a sense of complacency because they seem like such straightforward questions. The simple truth is that they all have the potential to sink your candidacy if your answers are not well thought out and on target with what the interviewer is really seeking to learn about you and your qualifications.

Understanding the Interviewer's Motives

No matter what words come out of an interviewer's mouth in the form of a question, what he or she is really asking is, "How will your background, experience, and personality contribute to the success of our organization?" Some interviewers may even explicitly ask that question at some point in the interview. However, in most cases, you will be asked any number of questions that probe your knowledge, your work experience, and your interpersonal skills in ways that the interviewer hopes will allow him or her to gauge your potential for success in the new position, as well as your ability to mesh or fit in with that company's culture. If you are aware of the interviewer's underlying motives, you can be better equipped to respond in ways that will provide the information needed for him or her to recognize you as a strong candidate with the right skills and personality to be a genuine asset to the company.

The 10 Questions You Need to Be Ready to Answer

Here are 10 of the most common questions you're likely to encounter in a job interview. They have been chosen because they're the ones that job candidates may provide weak answers for precisely because they seem so common and routine.

1. "Can you tell me about yourself?"

The common mistake in answering this question is thinking that the interviewer is asking for your life story. As fascinating as it may be, the interviewer is less interested in where you went to kindergarten and how you won the second grade spelling bee as he or she is in how your experience in your last job directly relates to this position. Limit your answer to work-related aspects of your background. Assuming that you've studied the job posting thoroughly and researched the company, tie your background and experience to the prospective employer's needs.

2. "Why do you want to work here?"

Again, if you've done your research, you should have some sense of what the company does, what the corporate culture is, and how your skill set fits into the picture. Your answer should be something along the lines of, "Your mission statement and corporate vision are consistent with my professional goals, and I believe my skills in the areas of [insert examples] will allow me to contribute to the success of [insert name of a specific program or a challenge the company faces]. The potential is very exciting to me."

3. "What do you know about our firm?"

Once again, research, research, research! If you can't tell the interviewer much about what the company makes and sells, or what its biggest challenges are, the interviewer may assume you have little genuine interest in the company or the position you're applying for. In this modern age, Internet access makes research relatively easy. Chances are, you found the job posting at a company Website, so be sure to explore the site in more depth to find out about the firm's products, plant locations, financial performance, and any other information that might be useful. If you're applying in the nonprofit world, many agencies have Websites that can provide information about the organization's mission, active programs, and funding. You may wish to refer back to Chapter 2, where we discussed researching prospective employers. Take note of the recommended resources mentioned in Appendix C, as well.

4. "What are your goals?"

When posed with this question, it's not a good time to share that your long-range plan is to own a sheep ranch in West Virginia. Your answer should relate to the job in question and perhaps how you see yourself within the organization three to five years down the road. Give some thought as to what the logical career path is for someone in your field, and tailor your answer to reflect that. Maybe that means aspiring to be a supervisor or manager within the department that hires you, or taking advantage of educational opportunities to enhance your value to the employer. Once again, if you've done your research, you should have some idea what's expected for an employee entering the company at your level.

5. "What are your strengths?"

Again, the real underlying question is, "How will your strengths fulfill our needs?" Choose one or more of your strong points and relate them to the opening you're being interviewed for. Your response could be something such as, "I've always been good with numbers, and I know that budgeting is a key component of this position. At my last job, I developed and administered a $580,000 operating budget and achieved all of our key objectives for the year while staying under budget." That might lead to a follow-up question such as, "Really! How much under budget were you?" To which you can reply, "We saved a total of $29,000, which was 5 percent." Notice how this second answer reinforces your assertion that you're good with numbers by demonstrating your ability to come up with the amount instantly and calculate the percentage on the spot.

6. "What experience do you have that's directly relevant to this position?"

This question is a variation of the previous one, so you can answer it pretty much the same way. Pick one of your core skills and explain to the interviewer how it will help you in performing the duties of the new job. For example: "I have extensive experience prospecting and cold calling while establishing long-term relationships. Because your firm sells capital equipment, I recognize that it involves a long sales cycle. I believe that my previous experiences will allow me to identify strong prospects and maintain a rapport with them over several months as we move them toward a buying decision."

7. "What would your former coworkers say about you?"

Your answer to this question can hurt you in two ways. First, a casual or flippant answer about how you get along with everybody will do little to advance your case with the interviewer. On the other hand, coming on too strong about how you have the professional respect of everyone you work with may sound a bit disingenuous. An even-handed approach might sound something like this: "I believe that they would tell you that I'm well-organized, consistently meet deadlines, and know how to engender cooperation among colleagues when necessary to meet objectives. They probably also would say that I have a great sense of humor and know how to defuse a tense situation with a small bit of humor, when appropriate."

8. "What are your salary expectations?"

This is a routine question that often comes up, but it's also one of the toughest challenges a job seeker faces. You may encounter this question because the interviewer is incompetent and truly doesn't know any better; or, the interviewer may be trying to gain a negotiating advantage by getting you to name your price first. If this question is broached in the early stages of an interview, the best approach is to say, "I think I'd like to know more about the responsibilities of the position and reach a point where we can agree that I'm the right person for the job before getting too deeply into salary discussions. As a well-regarded company in your industry, I'm certain that your compensation package will be in line with the current market and that we can reach a mutually beneficial agreement about salary." If the interviewer continues to press for an answer, you might ask what range they have in mind; whatever the answer, you should always be near the top of that range.

9. "Why should we hire you?"

Here's another great opportunity to talk about your key strengths as they relate to the job opening. An appropriate answer might be, "I have the skills and experience necessary to do the job, I believe in the company's mission and think its products are great, and I'm willing to commit to whatever additional training or education might be necessary to meet the department's future needs."

10. "Do you have any questions?"

This question may be the most important one you're asked in an interview. In fact, if the interviewer doesn't ask it, you should pipe up and say, "I have a few questions I'd like to ask." Either way, this is your golden opportunity to learn more about the company, the job, your role within the company, and more. Some interviewers say that the questions a candidate asks are often more important than his or her answers to the interviewer's questions. In addition to helping you gather information about the company, your questions can also demonstrate your interest in the position. An insightful question shows that you've done some research but are eager to learn more.

Tips From The Pros

Not all interviewers are going to come out and directly ask "What is your top strength?" Many will phrase the question in a number of different ways: "Tell me about yourself." "Why should we hire you?" "What would an old boss say about you?" "How would you add value to this department?" As you prepare answers to a list of standard interview questions, it is important to remember that a number of interview questions are designed to assess what differentiates you from other candidates— in other words, what are your strengths. With this in mind, as you prepare for an interview, you should identify your top two or three strengths as they relate to the position, and plan to get these specific points across to the interviewer during the interview. That way, when you are asked, "What makes you different from our other three candidates?" Twenty minutes into the interview, you can take the opportunity to address a key strength that hasn't been highlighted yet.

Laurie Berenson, CPRW

Sterling Career Concepts, LLC

One of the most common interview questions is "Tell me about yourself." People often have trouble answering this question because it is so open ended and they don't know where to start. The hiring authority is asking this question to determine your value-added and to decide if you are a good fit for the job. You need to craft a response that is crisp and to the point. Think of your response as if it were a PowerPoint presentation. Don't clutter the slides with too much information...just offer the key points. Here's what you should reference on your PowerPoint slide:

- Professional identity.
- Three core competencies and measurable proof of these competencies.
- Quick overview of your professional and educational background.
- The reasons why you are interested in the particular job opportunity or company.

Barbara Safani, M.A., NCRW, CERW, CPRW, CCM

Career Solvers

Many people feel uncomfortable bragging about themselves. The praise that you heap upon yourself may seem hollow or insincere. How do you convince the employer that you are indeed conscientious, creative, and highly organized? Doesn't everyone say they are self-motivated, dedicated, and hardworking?

Why should the employer believe you? During the job interview, as you are asked about your work experience, introduce your accomplishments by attaching them to a desired trait (Trait plus Achievement). For example, let's say you want to show the employer that you are highly organized. When you hear a question [and] your answer will require organizational skills, fashion your answer to state the Trait plus Achievement. You might say, "I am highly organized and this has enabled me to revise the filing system, making the files more accessible." The achievement you have tied to the trait will validate your claim to being well-organized. Some introductory statements may be: "I pride myself on being..." or "My supervisors have found me to be..." or "Colleagues recognize that I am..." Be creative in finding ways to state the traits that will introduce your answers.

Freddie Cheek, MS Ed, CCM, CPRW, CWDP, CARW

Cheek & Associates, LLC

In advance of your interview with a particular company, make sure you do your research. One of the first questions you will be asked is, "What do you know about us?" Your ignorance here will leave the interviewer with an unfavorable impression, and it's very likely your interview will be over quickly. At the minimum, you should know what products or services they provide, how long they've been in business, and their reputation in the industry. In recent years it has gotten easier to find this basic information [because] most organizations have Websites. To score additional points, Google the company name and you might find published articles that mention their initiatives in progress, changes in leadership, or other news-making events. The activities of smaller companies are often featured in the business section of newspapers, and these articles are usually archived. Log onto the local newspaper's Website, click on the relevant tab, and enter the search term for the company. There may be a nominal fee, but it is well worth it to arm yourself with information that proves you did your homework.

Melanie Noonan

Peripheral Pro, LLC

Other Resources

There are a number of excellent books on the market that address the questions discussed in this chapter, as well as countless others providing detailed sample answers and additional advice on developing your own answers to these questions. Several of them are listed in Appendix C, and we encourage you to consult them.

Chapter 8

▶ Simple Truths About Tough Interview Questions

Savvy interviewers have a reason for asking each and every question during your interview. As we've discussed, sometimes these reasons are clear and self-evident; and other times, there are underlying objectives at play. The better you understand the real question behind the question, the more likely it is that you will satisfy the interviewer and present yourself in the most positive light.

A persuasive case could be made that any question asked during an interview can be tough if you aren't prepared with a well-thought-out response, and if you aren't able to think quickly on your feet under pressure. I've chosen 10 questions that candidates have found to be among the toughest—these are some of the most challenging questions out there. By considering these questions in advance of your interview and figuring out how you would respond, hopefully you'll also be better positioned to respond to other questions in the moment. As always, honesty is the guiding light; however, being honest doesn't preclude being prepared.

Remember: To ace an interview, the focus needs to be on *them* (the target position and prospective employer), not you! Your goal in the interview is to demonstrate with every response how you are the answer to their needs and challenges.

The 10 Tough Questions You Need to Be Ready to Answer

1. "What is your greatest weakness?"

The natural response is to admit to a genuine personality flaw or negative tendency, period—for example, "I have a really hard time getting out of bed in the morning, and am frequently late." This level of candor can quickly torpedo your candidacy. However, it is possible to respond honestly without hurting yourself.

Just a few short years ago, the sage advice on how to respond to this question was to confess that you are impatient with lazy people—that is, coworkers who don't give 100 percent all the time (as you do). The other highly recommended approach was to respond by admitting that you are a perfectionist—which, of course, actually turns out to be a tremendous benefit to the organization. You're a martyr, consistently doing whatever it takes to get the tasks done correctly, under budget, and on time, no matter the personal cost. The trouble is, these responses became a little too common. Even if they were true, they strained credibility a bit, depending on the person and the circumstances. If you are, in fact, a perfectionist, you may choose to respond in this manner. In general, however, it's best to avoid personality traits here. After all, personality traits are extremely difficult to change, and your goal is to demonstrate that you are working on improving your "weakness."

Consider the question from the prospective employer's point of view. The underlying concern is that you have some type of serious character flaw. The interviewer's hope is that you will simply blurt it out in the heat of the moment, under the pressure of the interview situation. Don't do it!

The strategy of identifying a weakness rather than a character flaw, and then pointing out its positive aspects, is a sound one. It's also important to place the weakness in your past; you have conquered it! Here's an example:

"Although I tend not to dwell on weaknesses, I'm human, and I have limitations just like everyone, so I constantly strive to improve myself to become an even more effective worker. I used to become frustrated when the work of others negatively impacted progress on my own projects. Now, I've come to understand that everyone has unique contributions to make, and I offer to assist coworkers with challenges they encounter in order to expedite or improve overall progress, whenever appropriate. I've learned that working cooperatively in the spirit of teamwork ultimately creates a better, more profitable result for the company."

2. "How would you describe your personality?"

Here is another instance in which your research on the organization and target position is key to responding with a strong answer. Choose a few characteristics that genuinely describe you and also mesh with what you have learned about the prospective employer's expectations for the position. Think about traits of the ideal candidate, either based on what is listed in the job description or what the interviewer has shared. Your goal is to portray yourself as someone who can hit the ground running and be a solution to the organization's challenges, all while sharing some honest information about your personality.

Following are some examples of areas to consider as you develop your personality self-portrait:

▶ Is working well in a fast-paced, high-pressure environment one of your strengths? Do you thrive on this energy? Most importantly, does this reflect the prospective employer's work environment?

▶ Do you prefer to work as an independent contributor, or as a team member? Which of these work situations do you thrive in? Most importantly, which reflects the prospective employer's work environment?

▶ Are you a natural leader? Do you thrive in leadership roles? Most importantly, does this position require leadership skills?

▶ Do you genuinely enjoy multitasking in an atmosphere of constantly shifting priorities? Do you thrive in this environment? Most importantly, does this reflect the prospective employer's work environment?

▶ Are you a highly effective communicator who is skilled in finding ways to express ideas to particular audiences? Most importantly, does this position require excellent speaking or writing capabilities?

These are just a few areas to consider in developing your personality self-portrait. This is really an elevator speech that is focused on your key personality traits, which also happen to be vital to succeeding in the new position. Adapt your elevator speech from Chapter 2 so that it highlights the personal characteristics that relate most strongly to your target position. Here's an example of a personality self-portrait:

"I'm an upbeat problem-solver who finds joy in learning new things. A quick study, I adapt well to changes and maintain my high-energy positive attitude that supervisors will tell you lifts morale and supports team spirit. In fact, I've found that I thrive in a dynamic work environment. I take pride in meeting deadlines and doing what it takes to get the project done correctly the first time, on budget. I'm known for my ability to quickly establish rapport and trusting relationships with people at all levels, both inside and outside the company. The truth is, I enjoy working with people, and this has enhanced my ability to achieve results throughout my career."

3. "Have you ever been fired?"

Clearly, this doesn't rate as a tough question if you have never been fired. If you *have* been fired, however, it's important to distinguish among the categories of firing. Take special care in choosing your words here. To many, being fired means that you were dismissed "for cause"—that is, for wrongdoing of some kind. If this is what happened and you are asked this question, prepare your answer with these points in mind:

▶ Accept responsibility for your action(s). Don't blame coworkers or management.

▶ Avoid degrading yourself, and refrain from sharing excessive details of the situation.

▶ Be sure to place the event in the past, and demonstrate that you have moved on.

▶ Find a way to share that you have learned important lessons from the experience that, in fact, make you even wiser and hence more valuable to future employers.

Here's an example:

"I trusted a colleague to follow up on a major project while I reluctantly left on a family vacation that had been planned literally years in advance. There was a breakdown in communication, the project was botched, and the account was lost. It was a tough call, but I understand the decision. I'm still on good terms with many of the managers there—please feel free to contact them if you wish. I learned valuable lessons about accountability and following through, and believe I'm a stronger candidate and more valuable asset to a future employer as a result of this experience."

Downsized or rightsized

In the previous example, the dismissal was based upon your actions (or lack of action). By contrast, if your position was eliminated because of some force of nature beyond your control, such as a merger, acquisition, closure, or workforce reduction initiative, simply explain the situation. Remember that it's completely inappropriate to express bitterness or assign blame to the former employer; it's equally important to refrain from acting as though it was your fault. Your delivery is all-important here: Simply and calmly relate the facts, and then bring the conversation back to your being the right person for the position, following the thread of what you have stated.

Leadership change

If you were let go because of a leadership change, this was likewise out of your hands, so calmly and briefly relate the facts: "There was a total changeover in top management that resulted in my being let go, along with a number of my colleagues." If you know how many employees were fired as a result of the management change, then state that figure. If it's more compelling stated as a percentage, then express it in those terms: "In fact, more than 30 percent of the company's workforce was let go during this period."

4. "Why have you been out of work for such an extended period of time?"

Usually the underlying concern here is that you may have some serious problem or flaw that has prevented you from securing employment more quickly. It's not uncommon for people to be "between jobs" for extended periods of time in the current economic climate. (By the way, the definition of "extended" is whatever the interviewer believes it to be. It's not worth arguing the point or trying to convince the interviewer that 10 months really isn't so very long if he or she believes otherwise.) Be honest, and, as always, refrain from blaming others or the economy. Accept accountability for your choices and respond in an upbeat, optimistic tone. Honestly and briefly relate the facts, which can then be connected to the expectations of the position. Try to identify at least one thing you did during the gap that makes you a stronger candidate for your target position. Following are three examples:

"I decided to take the time to find something fulfilling, which would be truly rewarding and a good fit. In the meantime, I've been sharpening some of my skills through some courses in Web-based marketing at Upstate Community College. I pursued a few job opportunities during this period and, ultimately, turned down offers, as I determined they simply weren't a close enough fit. It sounds like this position would be an excellent fit, and I'm sure that I could make a meaningful contribution to your success. You mentioned that you're looking for someone who has experience in new product launches."

"For years, I have wanted to travel through China. This interlude provided the opportunity to fulfill this lifelong dream. Because my partner was fortunate enough to be eligible for a sabbatical at the same time, we decided to take advantage of the opportunity. I find exposure to different cultures and people of different backgrounds to be simply fascinating and invigorating. My work schedule never permitted an extended trip such as this. I returned with a new appreciation of this great country of ours, as well as a connection to people on the other side of the world. You mentioned that you deal with suppliers in Asia. Although I'm not an expert, I now have an understanding of that culture that could prove helpful."

"I used this time to manage our move and get us settled into our new home. We had our eyes on a wonderful 19th-century farmhouse that had been on the market but out of our reach. I was able to focus on negotiating a much better deal than we anticipated. Because it needed some major work, I was

able to do many of the renovations myself during this period. I learned that my project management skills were definitely transferable to selecting and coordinating the contractors for the work I didn't do, such as the plumbing and electrical. It didn't hurt to be on-site while the contractors were working, either. I recall the job description listed project management as a key skill...."

5. "Would you give me an example of an obstacle you've had to overcome to get the job done?"

Here's an opportunity to review the success stories you developed in Chapter 2 and select one that is most relevant to the target position. The interviewer is really asking about your problem-solving capabilities. Keep the following points in mind:

▶   Be sure to describe the obstacle without sounding like you are bad-mouthing the former employer in any way.

▶   Illustrate the obstacle clearly enough for the interviewer to understand what was so challenging about it, but without spending too much time on details that don't strengthen your story, and which may prove distracting.

▶   Identify the personal characteristics and skills that allowed you to conquer the obstacle and accomplish the objective. Be sure that these characteristics and skills are relevant to your target position and directly connected to elements of the job description.

6. "Have you ever had a disagreement with coworkers or your boss, and if so, how did you handle it?"

The primary underlying concern here is whether or not, and to what extent, you are a troublemaker. The interviewer wants to know how you get along with your colleagues and bosses. Good communication skills are essential anytime there's more than one person involved in any endeavor, and things only become more complex as larger groups of people interact together. You need to demonstrate that you are level-headed, rational, and an effective communicator. Here are two examples:

"I've been very fortunate to have worked in places where my input and contributions were sought in order to finish projects on time and under budget. I am comfortable offering my opinions, but I'm always sensitive to others, and I never criticize a coworker—or anyone—in an open meeting."

"When something comes up that I feel strongly about, I ask for time to sit down and discuss the issue one-on-one, either with a coworker or manager. I'm actually looking for an environment where people work together to solve problems and strive to exceed the customers' expectations. Am I in the right place?"

7. "Why should we hire you?"

This is actually a cousin of the "greatest strengths" question; however, it calls for a direct connection between your value and the organization's needs. Do you see how the interviewer is, consciously or unconsciously, asking you to make the hiring decision easier? By all means, connect the dots for the interviewer! Your elevator speech is already prepared, and hopefully you've updated it based upon your research on this prospective employer and target job. Now, take a moment or two to breathe, and then link what you have learned in the interview about the target position's deliverables to what you have discovered or sensed the interviewer values.

Quoting coworkers or supervisors is a very effective way of offering additional relevant, positive information about yourself without sounding as though it's your own high opinion of yourself. Phrases such as "Supervisors have complimented me on my…" or "I'm told that I have…" can function as lead-ins to help you discuss the accolades you've received with your interviewer. Speak enthusiastically and with energy.

8. "What did you dislike the most about your last job?"

One universal simple truth that has appeared throughout this book is that it's never helpful to speak ill of former employers. However justified you may feel in criticizing them, these kinds of remarks ultimately do not strengthen your candidacy, nor do they reflect well on your level of professionalism from the interviewer's perspective. Whining about former employers suggests that you do not take accountability for your decisions. Save your complaints for close, trusted friends, and maintain an upbeat, positive demeanor in job interviews.

The interviewer's underlying motive here is to determine how good a match you are for the target position. How compatible are you with the organization? For example, if the new position calls for a great deal of travel, and you state that the aspect you disliked the most about your last job was that you had to travel often, what do you suppose the interviewer will conclude? You get the idea. Following are some examples:

"There really isn't anything that I can point to that I dislike about being a customer service representative. I feel so fortunate to have found a field that suits my talents and that I genuinely enjoy. You mentioned that this position requires a lot of time on the phone. Well, in my last position, I demonstrated that dealing with customers on the phone is one of my strengths."

"I liked pretty much everything about my job. Because you've pressed, though, I guess I would say that I'm seeking an opportunity where I can contribute even more to the success of projects. I'm especially interested in a planning and scheduling role, and from what I understand, this position requires someone with those skills."

"I've discovered that if you approach everything with an open mind and a positive attitude, and keep the overall mission of the company as the guiding principle, there really isn't anything that a strong, motivated team can't accomplish. I really feel fulfilled when I can contribute to a successful operation."

9. "What was your biggest failure?"

The interviewer wants to give you another opportunity to reveal a serious weakness, and also perhaps to learn more about if and how you overcome adversity. Briefly describe the failure, and focus on what the failure has taught you or reminded you, and how this realization has led you to improve your decision-making or problem-solving. Then, redirect the discussion to one of your subsequent accomplishments, demonstrating that you have learned lessons from your failures. A number of highly successful businessmen have been quoted as saying that they learned much more from their business failures than from their successes.

Absolutely refrain from choosing an example that enters the realm of personal issues such as marriage, bankruptcy, or the misdeeds of a relative. Choose an example from the past, and be sure to make clear that the episode truly is in the past and that you have learned from it. Here's an example:

"To make extra money while I was in school, I accepted a job selling personal products through networking and home parties. I really was only looking for some extra money. A friend of mine said she was doing quite well at it, and thought I would enjoy the work, too. My research on the company indicated that it was reputable, with a solid line of quality products. Ultimately, I did make a little money, but had difficulty finding adequate time to really make a success of it. In fact, I vowed that I would never, ever take on another sales role. This is ironic, in light of my successful track record in financial and insurance product sales. I discovered that I excel at what I'm most passionate about, and I believe very strongly that everyone needs and deserves sound advice in these areas from experts with the utmost integrity."

10. "What is the last book you've read?" or "What is the best book you've read recently?"

The interviewer may be opening a window into your areas of interest away from work without asking the more direct, slightly-less-tough question, "What are your hobbies?" There may also be an element of trying to catch you off guard with an out-of-the-blue question.

Depending on your specific career field, the best impression may be made by choosing a current book on business, management, or self-improvement. Feel free to choose other areas, but you would be best served to be able to relate what you learned from the book directly to your work life. For example, if you strongly prefer not to choose a volume on customer service or team building, but rather insist on a New Age topic, be prepared to explain how the book's message has helped you learn to cope with stress.

It's not recommended to pull a title out of the air simply because you've heard of it, but haven't read it. Take care! The interviewer may well have read it. He or she may be eager to ask you follow-up questions, happy for the opportunity to discuss details of the author's message with someone else who has read the book. Also, choosing the hottest best-seller may sound disingenuous, especially if you truly haven't read the work and aren't prepared to discuss highlights or your impressions.

The book you choose will make a statement about you and your potential as an employee with the target organization. Choose carefully; avoid controversial authors and subjects (such as religion, politics, gender issues, and sexuality). The very best choices will be books that have somehow inspired or helped you to improve your skills or abilities, thus making you an even stronger candidate.

Tips From the Pros

All interviews will come with easy, comfortable questions and those that are a little more difficult (sometimes a lot more difficult) to answer. This is why it is so important to write out your answers to both easy and difficult questions. Writing down your answers forces you to think through the words you want to use and the thoughts you wish to convey. The more practice you have reading and saying your answers out loud, the more comfortable you will be during the interview. Practicing your answers for the easy and difficult questions will be your biggest asset in succeeding in any interview. It's not only what you are saying but how confident and prepared you are for the answers. Preparation is the key!

Kris Plantrich, CPRW, CEIP

ResumeWonders Writing and Career Coaching Services

Job interviews often generate anxiety brought on by personal doubts concerning any weaknesses or limitations that you may perceive, based [on] your credentials or background. Experienced job candidates will have established a prominent and well-substantiated employment record, but they still benefit from some interviewing practice and careful research of a company's history. Planning a solid interview strategy and doing thorough research will prepare you to handle even the most stressful questions. Exhibit confidence with strong voice projection, use your best English grammar, and smile and speak slowly while making eye contact with your interviewer(s). Take comfort in the fact that interviewers are trained company representatives who want you to succeed. You would not have been invited for an interview if they had doubts about your qualifications and your ability to meet their standards for the position.

Edward Turilli

AccuWriter Resume Service

Explaining why you've been fired can be one of the toughest interview questions you can face. Take heart: Lee Iaccoa was fired from Ford and made Chrysler one of the strongest auto manufacturing companies in the world. Stay focused on how you can solve the employer's problem. Explain the situation without bad-mouthing your former employer.

Makini Theresa Harvey, CPRW, JCTC, CEIP, CCM

Career Abundance

Always be honest when answering the harder questions and try to put a positive spin on unfavorable circumstances. Tell the interviewer what you learned from the experience, how you corrected the problem or mistake, and what you learned from having to correct the problem. Even the big issues like being fired will have something positive that came from it; you just have to identify, if you haven't already, what that was.

Kris Plantrich, CPRW, CEIP

ResumeWonders Writing and Career Coaching Services

Chapter 9

▶ Simple Truths About
Questions You Should Ask
the Interviewer

It's a startling revelation to some job seekers that, in today's market, it is not only perfectly acceptable for you to ask questions during your interview, but it has become virtually essential for you to do so. Why? Asking carefully thought-out questions can contribute significantly to your achieving two vital, no-nonsense interview objectives:

▶ Distinguishing yourself from similarly-qualified competition by demonstrating that you are well-prepared, genuinely interested, and sufficiently savvy and confident that you recognize that an interview is an opportunity for two-way communication.

▶ Learning more about the prospective employer and target position, which will help you determine if the opportunity is a good fit and if you really wish to pursue it further.

Recruiters and other human resources professionals have shared that when it comes to selecting the best person for the job, the caliber of a candidate's inquiries during the interview process often carries just as much weight as the quality of his or her responses to questions, particularly when competition is fierce.

Double-Edged Swords

Hopefully your research on the prospective employer is already well under way or nearly completed by now. Take care to avoid asking questions during the interview that concern a matter of public record—things that a serious candidate should already know about the company. It's nearly impossible to recover from asking such questions;

they can significantly harm or completely derail your candidacy. An example of such a question would be a job seeker asking an interviewer at Eastman Kodak Company, "So, do you folks still manufacture good old-fashioned film here?" Good questions demonstrate your intelligence and curiosity, and seek information not readily available via the Internet or other easily accessible sources.

The other side of the coin is equally dangerous. The old adage that nobody likes a know-it-all holds true in the job-search arena, too. Take care that you don't load your inquiry with so much data that the interviewer's eyes glaze over before you even reach the question mark! Overly detailed or obscure questions also run the risk of embarrassing the interviewer, particularly if he or she is from the human resources department and not an expert in the field. For example, the following question would definitely be judged as over the top: "I read that your new batch purification process takes into account the enhanced biodegradability of the polystrinacine-type components; however, isn't it also true that the latest EPA regulations require that waste products of this chemical composition be transported?" Trying too hard to make a favorable impression is just as perilous as under-preparing; find the balance that will show off your diligent preparation without offending the interviewer in either direction.

Timing, Turnabout, and Tactics

Consider carefully the timing of your questions, too. It's wise to restrict your inquiries to issues directly related to the employer's needs during an initial interview and prior to a job offer being extended. Questions about the position and the organization fall into this category. Hold off on questions about salary, stock options, bonuses, medical benefits, tuition assistance, vacation, scheduling, overtime, parking, public transportation subsidy, and any other "self-interest" areas until after a job offer has been extended to you.

Ideally, at least some of your success stories will lend themselves to a "turnabout" question at the end (a turnabout question asks the interviewer to comment on a topic from the prospective employer's viewpoint). Consider the following example. A candidate, Serena, tells the interviewer about how she successfully implemented a computerized system for managing reservations of company conference rooms: "My project resulted in reducing the time spent by support staff in coordinating meeting space reservations from an average of 16 hours per week to just four, which ultimately allowed the reallocation of several part-time employees to higher priority, more profitable activities. Our cost savings totaled approximately $24,000 annually. Would you say there are similar challenges facing your administrative staff here?"

Be sensitive to your timing of questions within the initial interview. Before beginning to ask questions of your own, make sure that you verify your competency for the target position and have a reasonable sense that the interviewer believes you have all it takes to do the job. Usually, once the interviewer has established in his or her mind that you are qualified for the position, there will be more openness toward responding to your questions.

In general, the more senior the target position, the more questions you can ask; in fact, it's almost expected that candidates interviewing for senior-level positions be fully prepared with compelling, targeted questions of their own during the interview. For the rest of us, more general questions are appropriate for human resources representatives, with more detailed, content-related questions reserved for managers and direct supervisors. Take care that you postpone more probing, detailed questions until a second or even third interview; avoid appearing presumptuous or overly aggressive too early in the process.

Remember, every situation is unique, and no single question is appropriate in all circumstances. As you develop your questions, have the position description and other research findings handy. Be mindful of the position your interviewer holds in the organization—is he or she an HR person? Your prospective direct supervisor? The department manager? A recruiter? The owner?—and adapt your questions accordingly.

Any Questions?

The following sample questions are intended to guide you and spark your thinking. Adapt them to your own unique circumstances, taking into account your target position(s) and research results. Again, take special care not to ask questions that are self-evident or that are covered in the position description or background on the prospective employer. As a general rule, ask no less than two and no more than four questions. Be mindful of the time allotted for your interview, and be sensitive to cues from the interviewer that you need to wrap things up. Typically, near the close, the interviewer will ask if you have any questions—that's your cue! Consult your prepared questions, and quickly choose the most relevant or pressing ones, factoring in what has already been shared in the interview. Here are some sample questions:

> ▶ What would you like to see accomplished by your department in the next three to six months?

> ▶ How would my work in this position support these objectives?

> ▶ How do you measure success?

> ▶ If I'm selected, what would be my two or three highest priority deliverables in the near future?

> ▶ Where does this position fit into the organizational structure?

> ▶ To whom would I report? If the answer is someone other than the interviewer, ask, "When may I meet that person?"

> ▶ To what extent is travel required?

▶ How does this position impact the organization?

▶ What would you say are characteristics of a top performer in this position?

▶ Whom would I work with in this position internally? Externally?

▶ Why did you join the organization? How long have you been with the organization? What keeps you here?

▶ How soon do you anticipate making a hiring decision?

Revealing Hidden Obstacles: Making It Easy for the Interviewer

Interviewers sometimes have concerns that they are reluctant to explicitly address in an interview. There are many possible reasons for their unwillingness to ask you about them, including perceived legal vulnerability or simple lack of training in how to properly cover delicate topics. Your interview performance is analogous to a subtle sales presentation in which you are the product. Effective sales professionals are masters in the art of overcoming objections. Anticipating an interviewer's concerns (which can be done through research or by recalling prior experiences in overcoming some work or life challenge) is a first step. One approach is to bring up any doubts that you believe the interviewer may harbor and resolve them in a positive way, thus casting you in the best possible light. The goal is to eliminate the issue as a deterrent to your candidacy.

Let's imagine for a moment that your resume shows that you have changed jobs every two years for the past eight, and have relocated to four different states during this time period. Let's further imagine that the interviewer doesn't ask you about this, yet you sense that it may be a concern. Frequent use of the terms "stability" or "longevity," and/or emphasis on the learning curve and significant investment the organization makes in its employees, may combine to alert you that you need to take charge. Learn when to trust your instincts; they are usually on target.

Consider the following example of a candidate introducing a difficult topic herself in order to ensure there is no lingering doubt in the mind of the interviewer after the session:

"If I were interviewing me, I'd probably wonder why I've moved so frequently and changed jobs so much. Well, my husband was in the Navy and was transferred frequently. Being a military family has been very challenging; however, he's now in a civilian position where he hopes to remain for the foreseeable future. We chose to return to this community where I grew up, because much of my family is still here. We have a great support system and

childcare is not an issue, thanks to several reliable family members who adore caring for our kids."

If you really want to pursue the job, sometimes the most effective approach is to do a bit of the interviewer's work yourself and address any perceived concerns head on. It's the surest way to clear the air of unspoken worries. Even if you were wrong, and the interviewer was not, in fact, greatly concerned, you have still eliminated such issues from the list of things that may haunt you later in the process.

Further Along the Garden Path

Once you have been invited back for a second or third interview, the level of rapport and trust that you've hopefully established with the interviewer makes it appropriate to ask more intensely focused questions. Again, be mindful of the participants (will you be interviewing with someone new?) as well as the nature of your target position within the organization. Adapt your own questions accordingly:

▶ Is this a newly created position?

▶ How is it that this position became open?

▶ Would the prior incumbent be available for me to speak with at some point?

▶ May I see an employee handbook/policy manual?

▶ If I am hired, what do you see as the key challenges I would face in this position during the next few years?

▶ What is the company's vision?

▶ What ongoing training or development do you like to see in employees? What resources are in place to support this?

▶ What do you see as this organization's greatest asset?

▶ May I have a tour of the building/facility/grounds/client's site?

▶ Which employees would be reporting directly to me? What do you perceive they need most from their supervisor?

▶ What kind of feedback/assessment systems are in place?

▶ Who will make the final hiring decision? What is the timeline?

Post-Offer Questions

Following are questions most appropriate to ask the decision-makers after an offer has been extended:

▶ To what extent is the work schedule fixed or flexible?

▶ How imminent is future relocation?

▶ What is your greatest frustration with how things are currently managed?

▶ Where would my workspace be located in the facility? May I see it?

Specific discussion of salary negotiation can be found in Chapter 11.

Tips From the Pros

Never tell the interviewer that all your questions have been answered; use the opportunity to learn more about the position and the company—and further impress the interviewer. Since most of the interviewer's questions will focus on your knowledge, skills, and abilities (KSAs), make sure your list includes some questions that do not relate to those areas. Following are some sample questions; limit what you ask to three so as not to prolong the interview:

- You asked a lot of questions about process improvement. Tell me more about the specific expectations you have for the successful candidate in this area.

- How do you measure an employee's performance and provide feedback?

- If I am the successful candidate, what would you like to see me accomplish during my first 30 days on the job?

- Do you foresee any significant changes in the company?

- Are there specific problems or challenges an employee would face in this position?

- Will I have input in determining my objectives?

- Is there anything else I should know?

Daisy Wright, CDP, BA

The Write Career Solution

Asking questions at the end of an interview gives you one more chance to market yourself. Always ask questions! A candidate who tells the interviewer [that] he/she doesn't have any additional questions comes across as disinterested in the opportunity. From the employer's perspective, a candidate who is seriously assessing a job will have follow-up questions. Candidates should ask a minimum of two questions, even if they are to confirm what was already discussed. Ask what the characteristics are for the ideal candidate. Listen attentively to the answer, and then respond by drawing parallels to your own experience. This allows you to make a connection between yourself and the ideal candidate, using the interviewer's own words. For example, if the employer answers your question with something like, "We're looking for someone who can stay on top of the budget, [who] has advanced Excel skills, and who could help us with next quarter's system conversion." Your response could be something like, "That's great to hear. My background seems like a perfect fit; I've handled detailed budgets for the last four years, have always been the go-to person in my group for Excel macros, and have experience working through a computer system conversion."

Laurie Berenson, CPRW

Sterling Career Concepts, LLC

An interview is a two-way process. It usually takes several months to pick up on office dynamics or to determine what your new position with the organization is really like. The following question is an excellent way to gain insight into a position and is helpful in deciding whether or not a position or company is the right fit for you: "What is one thing that you know now that you wish you had known when you first started?" Gaining as much knowledge about a position [as possible] is critical, and the above question may prove beneficial to you in your decision-making process.

Connie Hauer, BES

CareerPro Services

Don't hesitate to ask the interviewer for clarification to avoid misunderstandings that could be disastrous down the road if you are hired. If the interviewer seems to evade your general questions, continue to probe tactfully until you get satisfactory answers. You should know enough not to ask self-centered questions about salary, vacation, or benefits in an initial interview, as these topics usually will be addressed by the prospective employer later in the process. Inquiries about specific work schedules or overtime should also wait, as they may paint you as someone who is inflexible or inordinately concerned about these issues. Your objectives in the interview are to sell the prospective employer on making you a job offer as well as to discern if the position is a good fit for you.

Melanie Noonan

Peripheral Pro, LLC

Chapter 10

▶ Simple Truths About
Handling the 5 Toughest Challenges in a Job Interview

Let's face it: For most of us, the entire job-search process, especially anything remotely resembling an interview, presents challenges of one kind or another. We've already explored a range of interview questions, and you've had the opportunity to develop your own unique approach to handling such questions in order to demonstrate that you have what it takes to meet the prospective employer's needs and exceed expectations. Hopefully, by now you're beyond the initial, purely terrifying realization that the rest of your career may depend upon your performance in a high-pressure situation with a stranger whose judgment may determine whether you take the next step toward realizing your professional goals.

Now it's time to address the simple truth that some challenges are, in fact, more daunting than others. Perhaps you have noticed that the word "challenge" has found its way into the vocabularies of many people as a euphemism for "problem" or "any really tough thing." Some experts encourage using this term in order to refrain from characterizing anything as truly difficult or complicated or just plain tough to handle. Well, let's be honest: The five situations we're about to address can be truly challenging. With proper preparation, however, these situations can be navigated successfully. It is possible to accept the "lemons" that are thrust upon you and make the proverbial lemonade—that is, to find ways to transform this initially sour fruit into something pleasant and, yes, perhaps even sweet. How can you turn what seems to be an insurmountable obstacle into another opportunity for you to shine and demonstrate your unique value to the prospective employer? Let's begin.

Challenge #1: The Incompetent Interviewer

There are many possible explanations for an interviewer's incompetence, but there are no acceptable excuses. Rather than whine and complain, rage against the Fates, or harshly judge a fellow human being, let's keep our eyes on the goal: determining if the position and organization are a good fit for you and, ultimately, getting the job offer. The more skilled you are at identifying and understanding "incompetents," the more likely you'll have a positive outcome in spite of the interviewer's failings.

Most often, an incompetent interviewer simply has not been properly trained in effective interview techniques, and lacks the natural ability and intellectual prowess to perform appropriately in this context. Generally, to be a skilled and effective interviewer requires high-quality training and a fair amount of experience. In some cases, employees with superb capabilities in their respective areas of expertise are given interviewing responsibilities for which they are simply ill-prepared. Whatever the cause, it's vital to know how to recognize and then redirect such circumstances to your benefit, to the greatest extent possible. Essentially, this will require your taking control of the interview without the interviewer being aware of it.

Irrelevant questions

One manifestation of an incompetent interviewer is irrelevant questions. The interviewer may simply fail to ask you questions that provide you the opportunity to respond with answers that demonstrate your readiness for the position. If you sense this is happening, and it doesn't change as the interview progresses, it's time to call to mind your research and preparation. Thanks to your research, you will already have some information about the organization and the position; as such, you'll have a fair idea of the characteristics and qualifications required to succeed in the position. In this scenario, find a way to gracefully initiate discussion of your own applicable skills and abilities. Ask the interviewer questions to illustrate your readiness to succeed in the position.

For example, if you're interviewing for a position that requires strong attention to detail, you might ask, "Based on my research, it seems that this position really requires a candidate who is highly detail-oriented—would you agree?" Hopefully, the interviewer will pick up on your cue and respond in the affirmative. He or she may even be relieved! This is your opportunity to launch into one of your success stories about a position you held or a situation you faced in which your own attention to detail helped the organization or otherwise saved the day.

The disorganized interviewer

Just about everyone can claim to be overburdened by too much work to accomplish in too little time, with more piling up each day. Even if the interviewer hasn't had the opportunity to comprehensively review your documents, hopefully he or she will have them in hand when you walk through the door. Sometimes, in spite of the best intentions, your documents or some other key item (perhaps an annual report or recent spreadsheet) will be elusively floating somewhere on top of the interviewer's cluttered desk. Stifle showing any indications of your impatience or exasperation. Instead, while the interviewer excavates the archaeological site on his or her desk, gather your thoughts and relax. You have the advantage! This frantic search often serves as an additional icebreaker, and the interviewer's apologies can help you feel as though you are on more of an equal footing, as suddenly your "judge" has proven to be all too human.

If it turns out that the interviewer simply can not locate your documents in spite of searching everywhere, you may gently offer that you have brought additional copies as you produce a fresh set from your portfolio. Thus, you have demonstrated that you are well-organized, and your demeanor is one of humble helpfulness rather than vindictive superiority. If this is handled well, the interviewer will be genuinely appreciative and favorably impressed with your generous spirit.

The distracted interviewer

Ideally, an interviewer will keep the time allotted for your session sacred by rerouting incoming calls directly to voicemail or to another employee, and, certainly, by disallowing other people from walking into the office during the session. In practice, however, both of these interruptions can occur. Fear not! If necessary, jot down on your notepad where you were in the discussion when the interruption occurred. When the interviewer's attention returns to you, calmly carry on the conversation from that point. The interviewer will be favorably impressed with your poise and memory, even if you had to use your notepad.

Note that although both distracted and disorganized interviewers deal with their own respective issues, you have several opportunities:

▶ Carefully observe the office surroundings. You may notice something of mutual interest (perhaps a photograph, sports trophy, book, or magazine) that you may compliment or comment on, thus spurring a positive exchange with the interviewer.

▶ Relax. Take several deep breaths and use this unexpected "space" to calm your nerves and center yourself.

▶ Gather your thoughts. Prepare your response to the question at hand, and, based on how the interview has progressed thus far, determine what points you still need to make and how best to work them into the discussion.

Pronouncements and closed-ended questions

Closed-ended questions require only a yes or no in response. If you allow yourself to fall into this trap, the interviewer will simply check off a list of requirements, and there will be precious little opportunity for you to fully reveal your unique value. This scenario definitely calls for you to take charge—without appearing to wrest control from the interviewer.

One effective approach to mastering this kind of question is to imagine that the interviewer is really asking you for a concise but thorough response. For example, "Have you supervised 35 people?" becomes "Have you supervised 35 people? Tell me about it," and "Are you detail-oriented?" becomes "Are you detail-oriented? Give me an example."

Interviewers who ask closed-ended questions often also throw in pronouncements—declarative sentences that seem to require no response from you at all. If there is an adequate pause after one of these pronouncements, use it to your advantage. Agree with the statement (if you do agree) in such a way that it's clear you truly understand the interviewer's point; then, connect it to the position you're targeting. For example, if the interviewer says, "These are tough economic times. Tough, tough times," you may respond by saying, "Yes, they certainly are—and it seems that this position calls for someone who has a good track record in identifying opportunities for cost savings. While I was at XYZ Corp...."

The dissatisfied and disgruntled interviewer

In this scenario, the interviewer mistakes the interview session for an opportunity to share his or her pain, and proceeds to explain his or her frustrations with various aspects of working at the particular organization. Continue to appear attentive by maintaining eye contact and nodding appropriately, and when there is a pause, be ready to spring into action to refocus the conversation. State that you appreciate hearing the background on the organization because it helps you visualize how this position contributes to the big picture. This information also helps clarify how valuable your attention to detail (or your excellent communication skills, or your proven supervisory experience—whatever skill or experience is most relevant) would be for success in the position. Then, ask if the interviewer could identify some of the other key aspects of the job. This approach refocuses the discussion to what should be the matter at hand (your qualifications for the position) while also appearing to be responsive to the interviewer's comments (by characterizing the interviewer's personal complaints as "background").

Sharing too much

I believe that most people are honest and ethical at heart. As such, our instincts direct us to be naturally truthful in responding to questions. And it is absolutely my belief that it is never acceptable to state a falsehood. However, there may be times during an interview when you feel compelled to share personal information that is really not appropriate or required at this stage in the process. For example, perhaps the interviewer shares highly personal information about him- or herself, either in a deliberate attempt to elicit analogous information from you or simply because he or she customarily shares such information freely and without regard to propriety. Or, perhaps the interviewer arrived extremely late for your appointment, and by way of explanation, launches into an extended description of a highly personal situation. Whatever the cause, be mindful that it is neither required nor wise for you to reciprocate by revealing information that may impact your future job performance.

None of us can predict the future with 100-percent accuracy, and even my own crystal ball shrouds itself in mist when it comes to the following examples, which should not be shared with interviewers. Although they are not speculative regarding the future, the first two examples imply that you are unwilling or unable to effectively manage household operations, and so are also best left unsaid.

▶ "Yes, I know exactly what you mean. Our babysitter is late all the time, and it's so irritating."

▶ "Oh, yeah, my car quits all the time, too. Just last week, we had to be towed twice!"

▶ "My husband and I plan to start a family in the next five years or so."

▶ "When our kids get a little older, we'd love to move back to Madison, where my family still lives."

▶ "My wife's job may require that we relocate to D.C. sometime in the next three years."

▶ "I may need knee surgery if my physical therapy regimen doesn't work."

The best prevention for falling into these kinds of traps is to begin a job search only when you're truly ready. Take all necessary steps to ensure that you have reliable transportation and dependable childcare arrangements in advance of your job search. As for the rest, if you know for certain that you will have surgery or some other medical treatment that will require recuperation, wait until you're back in action to initiate your search for a permanent, full-time position. Your partner may not get that promotion requiring possible relocation, and you may not move back home in the foreseeable future, after all. In general, refrain from mentioning something that may not even come to pass, as it may unnecessarily weaken your candidacy.

Tips From the Pros

Understand the Question

There is nothing worse in an interview than answering the WRONG question! That is, answering the question you "thought" was asked. Inexperienced interviewers are more likely to ask questions that may be vague, indecisive, long-winded, multi-segmented, or otherwise poorly phrased. It is up to the interviewee in these cases to take charge in a subtle way and help guide the interviewer. When in doubt about the question you were asked, use one of these four techniques to buy yourself some time and get more information about what the interviewer is really asking:

- Ask the interviewer to repeat the question.

- Ask the interviewer to rephrase the question.

- Paraphrase the question back to the interviewer using different words to confirm your understanding.

- Ask the interviewer a clarifying question:"Did you want information about my last job or all my jobs?"

Once you understand the question, respond in a way that shows that a) you have the skills and credentials to do the job right now, and b) you fit in with the culture of the company or department.

Gail Frank, NCRW, CPRW, JCTC, CEIP, MA

Employment University

Challenge #2: Illegal Questions

A simple truth about illegal questions is that interviewers sometimes ask them because they are utterly unaware of the laws governing inquires. Ignorance of the law is no excuse for breaking the law—just as the police officer says when you claim not to have seen the 35 m.p.h. sign while cruising along at 50 m.p.h. However, as noted in the prior discussion of incompetents, someone who is thrust into the role of interviewer may simply be inadequately trained, but may still be trying, to the best of his or her ability, to look out for the employer's best interests.

In handling such questions, there is a broad spectrum of possible responses. At one extreme, you could confront the interviewer by pointing out that the question is illegal, express your outrage that you would be asked such a question, and state that, as a result, you no longer have any interest in exploring employment opportunities with the organization. Clearly, this approach effectively closes the door on future employment with this organization. Is that really your wish at this point in the process? At the other extreme, you could simply answer the question directly, which may well involve revealing information that could be damaging to your candidacy. Do you really want to risk losing the opportunity for a job offer at this time? Most often, it's best to chart a middle course. Keep your options open for as long as possible, and don't close any doors until you truly have enough information about the position to determine whether or not you want to continue pursuing it. You can always turn down a job offer after you have gleaned as much intelligence from the experience as possible.

Another simple truth about illegal questions is that, most often, they reflect an underlying concern that the interviewer wishes to probe. If you can figure out the question behind the question, you can then find a way to allay the interviewer's genuine worry. Accomplishing this without an indignant confrontation avoids embarrassing the interviewer, and may preserve or even strengthen your candidacy. Although you may be well within your rights to protest an illegal question and create a stink, remember the goals of this first interview: to determine if the position and organization are a good fit for you and to get you to the point of receiving a job offer, which you may then accept or reject. Embarrassing or humiliating the interviewer or putting him or her on the defensive is not a recommended method to advancing your candidacy.

It may be that you find a particular question so offensive that you decide in the heat of the moment not to pursue employment with this organization any further. Before you cross the point of no return, though, consider the following:

▶ Finishing out the interview on a cordial basis may be a productive experience that will enhance your performance in future interviews with other prospective employers.

▶ If the offending interviewer is not your future supervisor, it may be well worth continuing with the interview. He or she may simply be an incompetent interviewer with whom you would have little contact once hired.

▶ There may be other current or future positions with this organization that would be of interest to you, and in which you would have little or no contact with this interviewer.

If you are truly offended enough to want to terminate your candidacy, maintain your professionalism. Graciously state that you are withdrawing your application for employment at this time, and remember to thank the interviewer for his or her time.

Following is a chart that lists several illegal questions along with related questions that are perfectly legal for an interviewer to ask. Note the subtle and not-so-subtle differences between the two. (Note that employment discrimination law is a moving target; by the time this book is published, applicable laws may have changed.)

Sample Interview Questions

Illegal	Legal
Where were you born? How about your parents?	Are you legally authorized to work in the United States?
How old are you?	Are you over the age of 18?

Sample Interview Questions (continued)

Do you have any disabilities?	Could you please demonstrate how you would perform these job-related tasks?
Have you had any serious illnesses or surgeries? When was your last physical exam?	Are you able to perform the tasks essential to this position?
How many children do you have and what are their ages? What are your childcare arrangements?	Would you be willing and able to work overtime and travel as needed for the job? Would you be willing to relocate if necessary?
What faith or religion do you practice?	Would you be able to work on Fridays, Saturdays, and Sundays as required by the position?
Have you ever been arrested?	Have you been convicted of a felony in the last seven years?
Have you ever been in trouble with the law in any way?	Do you have a valid driver's license?
Have you ever served in the armed forces of any other country than the United States?	In what branch or branches of the armed forces have you served? What training did you have?

In general, questions about age, health status, and medical history often stem from the employer's perfectly understandable concern as to whether a candidate is fully capable of executing the tasks required of the position. When interviewers ask questions similar to those listed in the left column of the chart, often what they really want and need to know is shown in the column on the right. In any case, if you are asked any of the questions on the left, it's best to reply as though you're responding to the question on the right and connect your answer directly to the responsibilities of the position.

By far the most effective approach to handling illegal, inappropriate, or awkward questions is to totally bend them to your benefit—that is, to answer the question that you *wish* the interviewer had asked on the same topic. This requires quick thinking on your part, but it can be highly effective in refocusing the conversation and showing you in your best light. The following tips provide two excellent examples.

Tips From the Pros

Parents often worry about being asked about their children during interviews. Some questions about your family are illegal, but happen anyway. Sometimes, candidates themselves accidentally open the door by casually mentioning their children. And sometimes, a parent might choose to include time spent as a full-time parent on a resume to explain a gap in employment. Whatever the reason for the topic of children coming up, a parent must find a way to calm the interviewer's fears. After all, most interviewers do not hate children. They are simply concerned that a parent, especially a single parent, will miss too much work when the child is sick or school is closed. When an interviewer asks, "Do you have children?" a candidate could rightfully tell the interviewer that the question is illegal—but this generally does not result in a job offer! It is better to answer the question briefly and positively, making sure to address the unstated concerns, which are, "How reliable is your childcare? Are you going to miss a lot of work?" A parent-candidate could reply with a confident smile, "Yes, I have two wonderful children who go to Maple Park Elementary and the YMCA After School Program. And we're very lucky that my parents live nearby—they adore the kids and enjoy spending time with them." Then, unless asked, don't discuss children again. Focus on the skills you can bring to the employer.

Heather Carson, GCDF, CPRW, JCTC

Second Start

Perhaps the question did not come out as the interviewer intended. Take a step back and consider the interviewer's motives. If the interviewer is given a chance to think about it, he or she might quickly recognize their error. Ask yourself these questions:

- How uncomfortable does this question make you feel?

- Does the interviewer seem unaware that the question is illegal?

- Does your gut feeling tell you that this illegal question is an interviewer's mistake, or does it indicate deeper problems with the company?

- Is this interviewer going to be your boss?

- If you believe the questions reflect the culture of the company, is this a place you want to work?

Tactfully ask for a clarification to give the interviewer enough time to pause and rephrase or strike the question. Example:

Interviewer's question: Are you from Central America?

Your question back to the interviewer: "Could you elaborate on your question as it relates to the job so that I can be sure to provide all the information you need?"

Interviewer's rephrased question: "The person we hire for this position will service our customers in Central America. Can you tell us what sales and marketing experience you have in this region?"

Murray Mann
Global Diversity Solutions Group

Challenge #3: Interviewing on Short Notice

"Be prepared!" What an overused phrase, but totally on target here because it's your best shot at putting your best foot forward in a job interview when you're contacted on short notice. From the moment you send out your very first cover letter and resume or make that first networking contact, you had better be ready! This means being fully prepared on all fronts:

▶ Have your elevator speech polished, ready to go, and practice it frequently so that it feels and sounds natural (not stilted or over-rehearsed).

▶ Practice role-playing with friends so that you're comfortable answering questions posed in various styles. Have one or more trusted friends take on the role of different personalities such as intimidating, disorganized, negative, and so on.

▶ Have at least one full ensemble ready to put on in a moment's notice (this includes cleaned and pressed clothing, undergarments, accessories, and polished shoes).

▶ Depending on the season and climate, have the appropriate outerwear cleaned and ready to go in a moment's notice.

▶ Dedicate a briefcase or portfolio for exclusive use in job interviews. Fill it with the essentials discussed in Chapter 5 (copies of your job search documents, breath mints, and so on) and keep it in a readily accessible place at all times.

▶ Have a cash stash that includes small bills and plenty of loose change to be kept exclusively for getting you to job interviews (for subway, bus, or cab fare; parking meter or parking garage fees; and so on).

▶ Prepare your telephone interview area and keep it set apart for that purpose.

> ▸ Make the extra effort to maintain a tidy vehicle interior throughout the duration of your job search. This may take a few extra minutes every day, but when a prospective employer walks you to your car unexpectedly, suddenly it will have been worth all the effort.

> ▸ Even if you haven't had the opportunity to complete research on your target employers, write out your primary goals for the interview—for example, the key message about your background and capabilities you want the interviewer to understand, and what you most want to find out about the prospective employer.

Especially in these uncertain times, employers and recruiters sometimes need to move quickly, so you should be ready to move quickly, too. Not all candidates who get the sought-after invitation to interview will be available or as prepared as you, so use this as another opportunity to set yourself apart from the competition.

Tips From the Pros

Follow the Rule of Three. A great practice to follow in interviewing, but especially when interviewing on short notice, is the "Rule of Three." Simply put, it means delivering an answer in three parts to any question that might demand more than a yes or no reply. Preface each part by saying "First," "Second," and "Third," or something similar such as "Finally." Here's an example:

Q: "Why do you want to work for us?"

A: "First, I know I can be of help to you in solving those problems you mentioned. Also, I honestly like your culture here; it's obviously added to your success. And finally, I would say that your new product line impresses me. I think it's a winner!"

With a little practice, it becomes easy to present answers that are concise, simple to construct as you go along, and simple for the interviewer to remember. Don't worry about each part being a perfect answer. Strive for plausibility, not perfection. As long as you're in the ballpark, you'll score a hit!

Pierre G. Daunic, Ph.D., CCM, CRW, CECC

Fast Forward Career Services, LLC

Be sure to have the traditional and behavioral interview questions with your answers thoroughly thought through ahead of time, and practice your responses. Be prepared! If absolutely necessary, you can *always* ask to change the date and time (to buy yourself a day or two) by saying, "I am very excited to interview with you; however, I am already booked tomorrow. Can you tell me what other dates and times are available?" If an alternative time is offered, great! If not, the decision is yours: If you really want a chance at the position, you may indicate that you will rearrange your schedule to accommodate the interview.

Marilyn A. Feldstein, MPA, JCTC, MBTI, PHR

Career Choices Unlimited

Challenge #4: Explaining an Extended Employment Gap

There are many valid reasons for having gaps in your employment. Some interviewers and hiring authorities automatically assume the worst upon their discovery. It's vital to carefully and thoroughly prepare to truthfully discuss employment gaps in order to ease the interviewer's natural curiosity and concern while placing yourself in the best possible light in relation to the expectations of the position.

Children

It's fairly common these days for a parent to choose to leave the traditional workforce following the birth or adoption of a child. It's helpful to be able to point to some way in which you kept your hand in your field during the hiatus, however. For example, did you take on a part-time volunteer assignment with an organization that was somehow relevant to your field, or perhaps take one or more continuing education courses to enhance your knowledge or keep your skills sharp and current?

Illness

If your employment gap is due to a serious illness, don't flinch when the interviewer asks about it. Maintain your composure and enthusiasm, and consider adapting the following response to your own unique circumstances: "Yes, I was on medical leave during that time period. My doctor was thrilled with my complete recovery, and I realized that full health is truly a gift. I discovered what I most value in life, and as a result, I am committed to pursuing excellence in work that I genuinely enjoy. My understanding is that this position requires someone with a strong customer focus and attention to detail. In my prior role with XYZ Corp...." Note that this response addresses the gap head-on, explains the true cause, omits the details, and gracefully refocuses the conversation back to the needs of the employer and the candidate's capabilities in meeting those needs. The case would be even stronger if the candidate had been able to take a brush-up course or two or participate in some type of volunteer activity.

Family issue

Perhaps your employment gap is due to the serious illness of a family member, and you left your job to fill the role of full-time caregiver. Depending upon the nature of your career, you may be able to draw on relevant activities during this time and make a meaningful connection to the target position that will resonate with the interviewer. For example, you may have settled an estate or handled other financial matters following the death of a terminally ill relative whom you cared for. If your career is in the field of financial planning, banking, or insurance, you can make a powerful case for having real-life experience that is highly relevant to your target position. Perhaps you managed a property or properties and supervised various contractors' activities or grounds upkeep—an activity that required transferable skills relevant to your target position. Remember to clarify that the crisis situation has now been resolved, and you are eager to return to the career that you have genuinely missed during this interlude.

Searching

If you have been looking for employment for a very long time, you are not alone. Characterize your unemployment period as one in which you have been reevaluating your career goals, and that you look forward to finding just the right fit. Emphasize that your commitment to your work is 120 percent, and you have been searching for a fulfilling position in which you could make a significant contribution to the success of the organization. Again, it helps if you have also engaged in self-improvement activities (attended college courses, acquired new computer skills, learned a foreign language, and so on) during this same period. Be sure to mention if you were given a severance package from your prior employer, and how it allowed you to become selective in your search for a good fit. Most everyone is aware of current economic conditions, so avoid blaming the career field or market conditions. Besides sounding negative, it may strike some interviewers that you are shifting accountability. Instead, maintain an upbeat, positive attitude, and emphasize your strengths as they relate to the target position.

Incarceration

It's far more preferable to initiate a discussion of a topic like this on your own terms, than let the interviewer find out about it later and jump to the conclusion that you were deliberately hiding something. Again, always bear in mind that the interviewer naturally may have underlying concerns—in this case, about the company's liability for potential future illegal activities, whether you will display violence in the workplace, whether you will attract to the organization other people convicted of similar crimes, or whether you will steal from the organization.

Remember the overarching simple truth: Always be truthful. However, it's best not to blame others, society, or the economy for your incarceration, as the interviewer may conclude that you have not accepted or will not accept accountability for your actions. Again, carefully plan what you will tell the interviewer, being mindful of conclusions that can be drawn from each point you make. Consider adapting the following to your unique circumstances: "Yes, I committed a felony some years ago, when I had a serious lapse in good judgment. I'm not at all proud of this. What I am proud of, though, is that I did exercise good judgment after this and was released early for good behavior. I took several college courses in [insert relevant course(s) here] and was chosen to lead several work teams. We always finished our assignments on time or ahead of schedule. I've learned many important lessons, and most importantly, I think, I understand that I'll have to earn your trust. I also learned self-discipline, and am eager to contribute to achieving objectives as part of a solid team. I feel that I have what it takes to excel in this position—you said you needed a team player who is a quick learner."

As with the other examples, notice that after explaining the employment gap, the conversation is redirected back to the employer's needs and the candidate's capabilities that directly relate to the position. It's vital to strike a balance between sharing enough to convince the interviewer that you earnestly have moved beyond the employment gap a better person, and not divulging information that is superfluous and would only serve to harm your candidacy.

The most compelling yet simplest truth about what may at first appear to be "tough challenges" is that they truly are opportunities in disguise, if handled wisely.

Tips From the Pros

Companies understand that long gone are the days of having staff that stay with one company 20 years or more. However, candidates still should be ready to explain employment gaps. Most of all, be honest. Ensure that your resume focuses on your unique promise of value and use your cover letter to explain the gap. If it was a prolonged period of time, focus on any job-related activities, including volunteer work, [that] you performed during that time.

Explaining Incarceration

If you were incarcerated, again, focus on your value to the employer. Hopefully you worked for the correctional facility. Your resume should highlight the work and accomplishments there. Be sincere, forthright, and honest as you explain that you did something illegal, you served your time and paid your debt to society, and now you want to contribute to society in a positive way. Get the wonderful book: *No One is Unemployable: Creative Solutions for Overcoming Barriers to Employment,* by Debra Angel and Elisabeth Harney.

Makini Theresa Harvey, CPRW, JCTC, CEIP, CCM

Career Abundance

Challenge #5: Premature Salary Discussion

Several of my colleagues who are experts in the field of salary negotiation claim that whoever first mentions a salary number—the interviewer or the candidate—is suddenly in the weaker position. In general, this is a fairly accurate assessment. Ideally, the salary topic should not be discussed until a job offer is on the table. You have everything to lose if your response isn't perfectly in tune with what the interviewer has in mind. A common question sprung by many interviewers early in the process is, "What kind of salary are you looking for?"

At this early stage, it is extremely difficult to respond to this question directly and honestly without a high risk of weakening or even torpedoing your candidacy. If you reply with a number that is too low (either because you are too willing to be underpaid, or are worried that asking for too much will price yourself out of the running), you actually devalue your abilities. A lowball reply may even raise suspicion about your motives or cause the interviewer to doubt your understanding of the position. On the other hand, if you reply with a number that the interviewer perceives as too high, you may, in fact, price yourself right out of the market and cause the interviewer to conclude that the organization can't afford you. Either way, you've hurt your chances to get a job offer.

To be fair, some interviewers deliberately introduce the salary question early in the process to instantly determine your level of experience and possibly save everyone time. Some interviewers want to determine early on whether you'll settle for the low end of the scale. Still others are truly "shopping" among candidates, believing they are acting in the best interests of the organization by seeking out the least expensive candidate available. The best scenario for you is when the interviewer or other decision-maker is prepared to pay whatever is necessary to hire the person identified as the best candidate to get the job done.

Because it's difficult to determine the interviewer's motivation when the question is broached prematurely, it's recommended that you gracefully defer a discussion of salary unless and until a job offer is actually extended to you. How can you accomplish this without appearing insubordinate, overly shrewd, or even cagey? Try adapting one of the following statements to your unique situation—perhaps they will spark your own approach to deferring the salary discussion until there's a job offer on the table.

> ▶ I'd be pleased to consider any reasonable offer. How about if we come back to the salary discussion after we've more fully reviewed the details of the position and what you're really looking for, and after you've had the chance to see the value I can bring to this organization.

> ▶ Before we talk about compensation, could we discuss more fully your expectations for the position and how my qualifications meet your needs?

▶   I really need some more information on your expectations for the position before I could speak with any certainty about salary.

▶   My top priority is finding the right opportunity and a good fit. Once we determine there's mutual benefit, I would be open to any fair offer.

▶   Compensation involves so many factors besides salary—for example, vacation time, medical benefits, and tuition assistance—that I would need to understand more about your overall compensation strategy and how this position fits. I'm sure if you decide that I'm the best candidate for the position, we could come to a mutually beneficial agreement.

The next chapter addresses salary discussions and negotiations in much greater detail.

Chapter 11

▶ Simple Truths About Handling Salary Questions in an Interview

The salary discussion is probably the toughest part of the job-search process in general, and the most challenging aspect of the interviewing process in particular. If you've been out of work for more than a few weeks, you may already be feeling the pinch, and are likely anxious to start drawing a paycheck. If your job search wears on for several months, you may legitimately be in dire financial straits and really need to start earning again. Employers know this and will use it to their advantage whenever possible. However, bear in mind that a concession of a few thousand dollars in starting annual salary now will follow you for the rest of your career, or at the very least throughout your tenure with this employer. All your future raises, bonuses, and other incentives will be predicated on the starting salary you agree to when you're hired. Therefore, anything you can do to improve your negotiating position and increase your initial salary with a new employer will pay dividends that will compound over the course of your working life.

Avoid the Subject (or, Let's Play Chicken)

Back in the 1950s when guys like James Dean and Marlon Brando were big stars, a rather dangerous game called "chicken" was part of popular culture. Two drivers would head toward each other in their hotrods, and the first one to swerve to the side in order to avoid a head-on collision was the chicken. Considering the potential for catastrophic results, how frequently this game was actually played in real life is somewhat uncertain, but for children growing up in that era, it led to many a quixotic tale and inspired more than a couple of Top 40 songs.

A somewhat less dramatic version of this game is played out every day in interviews for all kinds of jobs. A candidate meets with an interviewer, and they have broad, lengthy discussions about job requirements, skill sets, and relevant accomplishments, but whoever mentions the issue of salary first is the potential loser. Why? Because, as any shrewd businessperson will tell you, when one of the parties in a negotiation names his or her price, that person is at a distinct disadvantage. This same principle holds true in salary negotiations.

But we're not negotiating, it's just an initial interview at this point, you might think. Don't be mistaken. If the interviewer can get you to reveal your salary history or your salary expectations, you have given your target employer a tremendous advantage in any future discussions. Worse yet, you can be screened out as someone who's too expensive for the company to hire (if your salary number is too high), or as someone who's not experienced or sophisticated enough to handle the position (if your salary number is too low).

Most experts agree that you should avoid salary discussions during an initial interview if at all possible. You want to defer that conversation until you know more about the position you are interviewing for, and until you have a better handle on whether or not you even wish to work for the prospective employer.

When to Discuss Salary

An esteemed colleague, Jack Chapman, who literally wrote the book on salary negotiation (*Negotiating Your Salary: How to Make $1,000 a Minute*, Ten Speed Press) uses the terms "budget," "fudgit," and "judgit" when explaining the right time to discuss salary with your next employer. He goes on to use the analogy of buying a car that you can't afford. First, you start out by establishing your budget: "This is how much I can afford. That's my budget, not a penny more." Second, as you admire the car, you begin to waver and think, *Well, I really like it and if I go ahead and buy it, I'll figure out a way to pay for it. I can cut corners in other areas: no premium movie channels on TV; we only eat out once a month; maybe a more modest vacation for a couple of years*. That's the fudgit stage. Last, you enter the judgit stage, in which you carefully compare the value of the new car as it pertains to your lifestyle versus the cost of owning it. Perhaps some or all of the payment can be deducted as a business expense, and the car may even enhance your business opportunities by making you more mobile, or by adding to your prestige if it's a luxury model.

Applying this concept to your job search, the employer may start out looking to fill a position with a specific salary in mind: "This is what we have budgeted for this position." During the course of the interviewing process, you establish your unique value and cause the interviewer or hiring manager to start thinking, *This person could really make a difference for us. I wonder what her salary expectations are—I wonder if we can afford her.* Finally (hopefully for you), the decision-makers are so impressed that they start thinking, *If this person can do for us what she did for her previous employer, we could increase top-line revenues by $1.2 million and bottom-line profits by $150,000. With that kind of return on investment, she's easily worth $100,000, even though we only have $72,000 budgeted for this position. Of course, if we can get her for $85,000 or $90,000, all the better for us.* The employer is now mentally justifying hiring you at a potentially higher salary than what was originally budgeted. The higher salary would be seen as a good investment due to your perceived value and the employer's projected return on that investment.

If, during the first interview, the employer asks you, "What is your salary expectation?" and you volunteer that you would be willing to join their organization for a salary of $85,000, one of two things might happen. The employer may dismiss you as a candidate because your salary expectation is well above the firm's budgeted number ($72,000). On the other hand, the hiring manager may decide to continue talking with you, ultimately choosing to hire you because of your qualifications and demonstrated track record of success. Because you already stated that you would accept $85,000, more than likely you will get an offer between $75,000 and $80,000. You may be able to negotiate a salary in the low $80,000 range, but certainly not more than the $85,000 you divulged in the first interview.

If discussion of salary is deferred until much later in the process—perhaps during a second or third interview—you might receive an offer of $85,000 and be able to negotiate your way up to $100,000. Remember, in the previous example the employer recognized your value and was (in his/her own mind) willing to make an offer as high as $100,000 in order to hire you.

In another variation of this scenario, once you understand the responsibilities of the job and the employer's expectations of the person hired, you decide that you would only consider taking the job for a salary of $100,000. But you already mentioned the figure $85,000 before you knew all the facts, and now you're stuck. If the employer offers you $85,000 and you ask for more, of course he or she will say, "But you said you were willing to take the job at $85,000, and, frankly, that's a lot more than we were planning to pay. We're willing to meet your expectation, so when can you start work?" Even if you explain that the position is much more involved than you realized, and you therefore believe a higher salary is appropriate, you're at a negotiating disadvantage at the very least, and could very easily lose credibility with the hiring authority.

The bottom line on the question of salary is to defer that discussion as long as is reasonably possible; you should never be the one to mention salary first. Give yourself as much of an opportunity as possible to gather information about the job opening, while showing the prospective employer that you would bring exceptional value to the organization. When the employer inevitably asks you the salary question, be prepared with a well-thought-out response.

Knowing What You're Worth

Perhaps just as important as knowing how to defer salary discussions until the appropriate time is knowing what your value is when it is time to negotiate salary. Many factors go into determining what an appropriate salary is. First of all, you need to think in terms of total compensation, not just salary. Total compensation includes things such as paid vacation, medical and dental insurance, life insurance, vehicle allowance, 401(k) contributions, tuition and training allowance, and more. Depending on where you live, medical coverage for a family of four can easily exceed $10,000 per year in health insurance premiums. If the employer is paying for that in full, it may impact what your starting salary would be. The other benefits carry similar value that must be considered during such negotiations.

A word that appears many times throughout this book is "research." Just as you have been encouraged to research the company, its products, its business challenges, and its culture, you will also want to research salary and compensation issues before entering into negotiations with your prospective employer. Websites such as *www.salary.com*, *www.bls.com*, and several others listed in Appendix C are superb resources for determining what the average salary is for a particular job title in a particular city or region. Determining the average salary that an employer in your industry in your market will pay will give you a fair idea if the company interviewing you is on a par with other similar businesses. This information, along with other details of the benefits that are included, will help you decide what salary to ask for once negotiations start.

If you're considering relocating, you'll also want to explore the cost of living in the city in which your prospective employer is located. The costs of housing, food, clothing, gasoline, childcare, and just about everything else will vary widely from a large metropolitan area on the East Coast to a relatively small community in central Ohio, in Upstate New York, or in one of the Dakotas, for example. Salaries may be lower in less populated areas simply because it costs so much less to live in such places. On the other hand, places such as Alaska or Hawaii may have significantly higher costs of living because virtually everything from building materials to breakfast cereal must be shipped in from elsewhere.

The local chamber of commerce can be a resource for some of this information, as can the real estate section from the local newspaper. Many larger newsstands may well have newspapers from around the country, including one from the city or area where your target employer is located. You can also find volumes of information on the Internet. In addition, if you are invited to an interview and it's held in the area where you would be working, try to squeeze in a trip to the local supermarket to do some comparison shopping. Likewise, if time and circumstances permit, call a real estate agent to get a sense of what homes cost and/or what it might cost to rent an apartment that meets your needs.

One strategy is to take along your spouse or significant other and have that person check out the real estate market, supermarket(s), and perhaps the school system while you're busy interviewing. This can be a great help in gaining intelligence about the general lifestyle in the area. Also worth considering is what the job prospects are for your spouse in the new location. If you garner a 30- or 40-percent increase in compensation, but your spouse has trouble finding employment in his or her field, the salary increase may not seem so attractive.

All of this research will help you to decide on a figure that's going to enable you to make a move and accept a position with the new employer. This is simply one more compelling reason for delaying salary discussions for as long as reasonably possible.

What to Say if They Bring It Up First

Depending on the level of the position for which you are interviewing and how savvy the interviewer is, the prospective employer may pop the salary question early in your first interview, or it may not come up until a third or even fourth interview. Regardless of when it happens, most experts on the topic agree that your initial response should be something similar to this:

"Well, I know that your company has a stellar reputation and I'm pretty confident that I have skills and experience that will address your needs in this role, but I'd really like to learn more about this opportunity and have a chance to tell you a bit more about myself before we get into any discussions of salary. Assuming you feel I can bring value to your firm and assuming I feel like this will be a good fit for me, can we agree to table the salary discussion until a later time?"

This will most likely elicit one of two responses from an interviewer. He or she will either respect that answer (and perhaps even be impressed that you are savvy enough not to take the bait by answering the question), or he or she will reiterate the request. In the first instance, the interview will most likely continue and the salary question may well be deferred to a subsequent interview. In the latter case, the interviewer may come back at you and ask, "We really need to understand what kind of salary you're looking for, just so we're not wasting each other's time. So what are you really looking for, salary-wise?" Your response should most likely be your own version of this:

"I understand, and I agree that we shouldn't waste each other's time, especially if we're way off the mark. But may I ask you something? You must have a budgeted figure in mind for this position, or at least some range in mind. Would you tell me what you had in mind for salary, based on the responsibilities of the position and your stated requirements for someone with the relevant skills, education, and experience?"

This may put the interviewer on the defensive or make him or her feel somewhat uncomfortable. But it also puts the interviewer on notice that you're not going to be a pushover on the salary question. This is where the negotiating begins, and a seasoned and savvy interviewer or hiring manager will give you some kind of a range, for example: "We're hoping to place someone in this position for between $45,000 and $55,000." Whatever the stated range is, even if the lower end of the range is much more than your hoped-for salary, most interviewing coaches recommend one of the following responses:

"Well the higher end of the range is close to where I was hoping to be."

or

"Well, that's not exactly what I was expecting, but let's keep talking. I'm sure once we can decide that I am the right person for this job, we can agree on a salary that's fair and equitable."

In both cases, you're telling the interviewer that you're interested and that the salary range is reasonably close enough to your expectation to make it worthwhile to continue the discussion. At the same time, you've left yourself some wiggle room to negotiate when the timing is right.

Overall salary negotiations can be terribly complex. The overriding strategy for most job seekers should be to:

▶ Defer salary discussions until the employer has decided to make you an offer.

▶ Be sure to research the salary trends for your target industry, and be aware of the cost of living in all of the areas you may be relocating to.

▶ Establish in your own mind what "magic number" would make it worth making a move.

▶ Remember to factor in the complete benefits package when considering the total value of a job offer.

Appendix C offers many valuable resources, including entire books that are devoted solely to negotiating your salary. Consulting some of these resources will give you a broader perspective on salary questions and how to address them.

Tips From the Pros

Many candidates lose a job opportunity by negotiating salary too soon...and they don't even realize it. Once you quote a specific salary, you have started the negotiations. Even worse, you may have quoted too high, and they may already eliminate you. How to prepare? First, understand that salary is only one aspect of your total compensation. Determine in advance, what your total needs are including salary, vacation, benefits, commuting costs, etc. Decide where you are able to be flexible. How to answer? First, ask the employer what the salary range is for the position and you can then affirm (or not!) that the range is within your ballpark. Try to avoid further discussion about it until an actual offer is on the table. Second, you can quote a salary range that you are looking for, based on research; emphasize that you are interested in being paid fairly for the scope of the position, and that...the acceptable salary will be influenced by the rest of the compensation package.

Diane Irwin

Dynamic Résumés

Here are some tips on how to dodge the salary question if it comes up before you're ready:

- When an ad asks for salary history or requirements, write this:"I have always been fairly paid for my contributions and I will be happy to discuss salary with you when we meet."

- When an application asks the same, write:"Confidential" or"Will discuss."

- During an interview, say something like,"I always keep my salary history confidential for two reasons. First, I've never felt it right to divulge the salary scales of my previous employers. I am sure you can understand why. Second, I don't wish to be judged only on my past earnings."Then, since most employers already have a range in mind, ask them what it is. They might just tell you.

Pierre G. Daunic, PhD, CCM, CRW, CECC

Fast Forward Career Services, LLC

Your negotiating power stems from your ability to demonstrate how your contributions will increase revenue and productivity and/or decrease costs and stress for your employer. Therefore, the earlier you talk about salary (without having first addressed the employer's concerns), the worse your negotiating position.

- If prompted for compensation requirements **before the interview**, avoid giving a "ball park" figure. Instead say,"I'd like to find out more about this position and the needs of the company before we talk about salary."

- If probed for salary information **during or immediately following the interview**, politely decline by saying "I've learned a lot in meeting with you and I remain interested. However, I'd like some time to fully digest our discussion. Is Wednesday, the 12th soon enough to get back to you so that I'm still in the running?"

- If you're **pressured repeatedly** to give your salary requirements and you see no way around supplying an answer, try this: "I'm looking at positions that fall within the $55K to $65K salary range." This comment will satisfy the hiring manager's demands while leaving you with some breathing room to negotiate later.

Cliff Flamer, MS, NCC, NCRW, CPRW
BrightSide Résumés

If the prospective employer appears to be interested in you but discloses a salary range that is below your expectations, remind them of the value you will bring to their organization. If you had been listening carefully to the manager's spiel about their plans and goals, you should have picked up clues to their hidden agenda beyond the requirements of your target position. At this point, you can negotiate a win-win situation by bringing up what you perceive to be their unmentioned needs and convincing them that you have what it takes to address them.

Melanie Noonan
Peripheral Pro, LLC

Don't consider "salary" alone with deciding whether to accept an offer. Your decision should be based on the "total compensation package," which may include several of the following items:

•"Cafeteria Plans"	•Disability Insurance	•Car Allowance
•Medical Insurance	•Stock Options	•Expense Account
•Paid Vacation	•401(k)/Pension Plans	•Club Memberships
•Sick Days/Personal Days	•Life Insurance	•Professional Memberships
•On-site Childcare	•Relocation Expenses	•Flex Time/Job Sharing
•Telecommuting Options	•Tuition Reimbursement	•Employee Assistance Program

Gail Smith Boldt
Arnold-Smith Associates

Part III

▶ Post-Interview
Follow-Up

Chapter 12

▶ # Simple Truths About
Evaluating Your Performance

Objectively evaluating your interview performance is vital to developing your own unique style, enhancing and refining your future interview performance, and deciding on next steps in the process. Because the interview is also your opportunity to learn more about the position and the prospective employer, it's even more vital for you to evaluate what you have learned during the interview to help determine whether you wish to continue pursuing the particular target employer and position.

Self-Evaluation

To help you continue to learn and improve as you progress through your job-search process, it's a good idea to evaluate yourself after each interview experience. Rather than judging yourself too harshly, use this exercise to identify what went well in order to build your confidence and further enhance your performance in future interviews. Honestly consider what, if anything, you could have handled more effectively. Visualize what you wish you had done or said to place yourself in the most positive light. Replay in your mind the "ideal" behavior that you wish you had displayed, and then make notes to help you remember for next time.

You're the only one who will see your self-rating and your notes to yourself, so, in the spirit of continuous improvement, be as objective as you can. (See Appendix B for a blank form for you to copy and use for your own interview evaluations.)

Self-Evaluation Rating Scale

1 = needs improvement/not comfortable at all

2 = adequate/fairly comfortable

3 = nicely done/truly confident

Sample Interview Self-Evaluation

New Age Manufacturing, Inc.—August 1, 2008—Austin Sellars, VP Marketing and Sales		
Item	Notes/Ways I Could Improve in the Future	Rating
Arrived on time? Early?	Perfect!	3
Wardrobe appropriate?	Should have taken time to shine shoes, but no wardrobe malfunctions.	2
Good solid handshake?	Try to make and maintain eye contact during handshake	2
Good eye contact?	Was a little distracted by activities right outside the window, but overall, good.	2
Went prepared with all necessary info to complete company application if requested?	Forgot to bring along my reference sheet, but had memorized my references in preparing it, so was able to complete the application anyway.	2
Listened and responded clearly and articulately?	Yes!	3
Demonstrated my strong interest in and research on the organization?	Yes!	3
Clarified job expectations and how target position fits into the big picture?	I should have been more willing to inquire more closely about the reporting relationships; organization chart was very complex	2
Shared stories in response to questions that show past successes relevant to prospective employer?	Yes, but need to be more concise; probably described too much detail for time allotted. But interviewer seemed favorably impressed.	3
Overcame interviewer's objections to perceived obstacles to selection?	Explained that I'm only looking to leave my current employer after only one year due to the company's planned relocation out of market (across the country) and my desire to remain local, if possible.	3
Responded to questions with a positive attitude (without criticizing prior employers or shifting accountability)? What were the questions you found most challenging?	Yes! "Tell me about yourself." I need to polish my elevator speech!	3
Asked your own questions of the interviewer at appropriate time(s) and requested clarification as appropriate?	Again, should have requested clearer description of reporting relationships, but asked other questions I had prepared in advance.	2
Remembered to capture names and/or business cards from everyone you met?	Yes!	3
Remembered to thank the receptionist or other support personnel?	Shook hands with the executive secretary, but neglected to take the extra time to stop by the receptionist's desk on the way out.	1
Closed with expression of your desire for the position and your thanks to the interviewer(s)?	Yes!	3

The closer your total score is to 45, the better. Hopefully, by working through this exercise you have identified and reaffirmed your strengths, and have targeted areas in which you can improve your interview performance.

Evaluating the Opportunity

Remember that the interview is your chance to gather information about the target position and the prospective employer to help guide your decision about pursuing employment with that organization. It's important for you to objectively evaluate the opportunity in order to make a well-reasoned decision about continuing to pursue it and, ultimately, accepting an offer of employment.

Following are some suggested points to consider in this context. While not intended to be an exhaustive list, working through these items hopefully will spark your own thoughts on priorities to evaluate in determining whether a particular opportunity is a good fit for you:

Compatibility Rating Scale

A = Nearly perfect fit

B = I could live with this

C = Not a good fit at all

Priority Rating Scale

1 = Highest priority

2 = Mid-level priority

3 = Low priority

Sample Opportunity Evaluation

Item	Priority Rating	Compatibility Rating	Comments
Was the job content as anticipated or otherwise still to your liking?	1	B	
Did you learn new information about expectations such as travel, routine work schedule, or overtime?	1	B	Yes—didn't discuss in detail yet.
Will you have the opportunity to meet your prospective direct supervisor prior to a hiring decision? Did you connect in a positive way with this individual?	1	B	Yes, met briefly. Was told he would interview next round.
Do you feel positive about any colleagues you met?	2	B	Only briefly. Seemed nice.
Did the overall "feel" of the place seem appropriate/comfortable to you?	1	A	
Did the interviewer(s) respond to your questions openly and provide the information you requested?	2	A	
Did you learn new information about the organization's future plans that impact your level of interest in the position?	2	A	Just awarded big, new contract!
Did you learn anything new about the organization's history or status (such as pending lawsuits or recent or imminent policy changes)?	2		No news.
Did you have the opportunity to observe your work area? Was an opportunity to do so discussed?	2	B	
Did you learn anything new about your work location that impacts your level of interest in the position?	2	A	On bus route. Perfect backup for bad weather days.
Did you learn anything about additional training or education that may be required for your target position? How about availability and accessibility of professional development within the organization?	2	A	Great tuition assistance program!
Were the success criteria for the position reasonable in your opinion?	1	B	Great expectations!
Is this a newly created position? If not, did you learn why the incumbent or recent incumbent is leaving/left?	2	C	Sounds like there may have been "issues"—hope to learn more in future discussions.
Did you learn how the target position fits in to the big picture?	2	B	Hope to learn more.
Did you learn about potential future advancement within the organization?	1	B	Hope to learn more.

Now that you have completed point-by-point evaluations of your performance and the opportunity, it's time to take a step back and consider the entire interview experience in light of your reflections:

▶   Overall, what have you learned from this interview experience that you can apply to improving your performance next time?

▶   Based on the information you've gathered, along with your instinctive, intuitive reactions to the people, the environment, and the culture, do you wish to continue pursuing this particular opportunity?

▶   If yes, then what do you feel *really* good about in terms of the opportunity and the organization as a whole? Use this as the foundation for your post-interview follow-up.

Tips From the Pros

Evaluate your own performance, that of the recruiter, and the job fit: Envision yourself through the eyes of the interviewer. Answer the following questions immediately after the interview: Did you speak articulately and confidently? Has the interviewer left you with the feeling that he/she approves of you and is interested in hiring you? Did you make eye contact? Did you raise good questions for the interviewer related to the job specifications, the industry or profession, or the specific company? Did the interviewer convey comments that may have suggested interest or disinterest in you or your qualifications? After discussing this job and its responsibilities, do you believe you are fully qualified? Do you believe you will you be happy and successful if you accept an offer? Will you fit in comfortably? Do you envision at least adequate advancement if hired? Were you energetic in closing the interview to demonstrate your continued interest in being hired? Did you ask for or receive the interviewer's business card for follow-up contacts?

Edward Turilli, MA, CPRW

AccuWriter Resume Service

If you're being invited for interviews but you're not receiving job offers, your interview performance should be reviewed. Recognizing how difficult it is to analyze your own performance, the best way to do so objectively is by videotaping yourself in mock interviews. Prepare questions that have been asked of you during recent interviews, or choose some from this volume (see Chapters 7 and 8). Have someone conduct a recorded interview with you. While reviewing the tape, watch your non-verbal language. Are you confident in your answers? Is your voice strong and even? Do you make any peculiar facial or body movements that might be distracting? Address all areas and practice, practice, practice to correct any troublesome actions. Assess how you answer questions. Do your success stories demonstrate that you possess sought-after skills? Are your comments about past employers spiteful or derogatory in any way? Do you complain or blame others when answering questions? These and any other problem areas should be addressed and reworked.

Kris Plantrich, CPRW, CEIP

ResumeWonders Writing & Career Coaching Services

Don't be afraid to ask the interviewer how well you did, and if there was anything you could add that would help them choose you. Have an interview debriefing session with your career coach or someone else that you trust. Hopefully, you took copious notes. Review your notes for any issues or ideas. Some questions to ask in the debriefing session include:

- How well did I answer the questions?
- Did I present my unique promise of value in a compelling way?
- Was the job, the company, and my qualifications a good fit?
- Am I overqualified or underqualified?
- Do I lack the experience or education?
- What strategies should I develop to deal with the issues above?
- Is the salary in line with what I want?

Check if your values and priorities match. If you really want the job, be prepared to continue communicating with the company. If you decide the company is not for you, let them know immediately so that you can move on and the company can continue their search.

Makini Theresa Harvey, CPRW, JCTC, CEIP, CCM

Career Abundance

In an RHI Management Resources survey, executives were asked about the worst mistake management-level candidates make during an interview. Half (50 percent) said a showing of arrogance was the biggest turnoff. While confidence is important, showing too much confidence crosses the line into bragging. Growing up, many of us were taught that it was "wrong" to talk about your accomplishments. No one likes a bragger. However, sharing the things you are proud of is an important part of letting an interviewer get to know you. Successful job seekers know that explaining what they can do for a company is not "bragging" or "tooting their own horn[s]." John, a research director who has changed careers twice, explains the difference between bragging and sharing his experience. "I keep my focus on sharing facts and stories without embellishments or value judgments. It is simply sharing the data. If the focus is on you, then it might be bragging. If the focus is on the benefit for the company, your boss, or workgroup, then it is enlightening others." As a savvy interviewee, you can share the facts, details, and results of your efforts in a way that helps the listener relate your past successes to their own unmet business problems, needs and challenges.

Gail Frank, NCRW, CPRW, JCTC, CEIP, MA

Employment University

An excellent evaluation tool that should be part of your job search toolkit is an interview tracking method. Keep track of all your interview sessions, contacts and referrals on the wonderful job search and career management tool at *www.jibberjobber.com*. Founded by Jason Alba, a jobseeker who wanted an organized way to manage his job search, [this site] is an excellent tool for tracking all of the information that you collect during a job search. You can track companies that you apply to, each job that you apply for and the status of each interview, including the first interview date, correspondence sent and received and more. Because it is Web-based, you can include as much information about the interviews as you need. Include important things such as the tone of the meeting, positives and negatives about you, the position, the company, and more. Include any important issues you need to address and any questions you still may have for the interviewers. Write your draft thank you and follow-up letters; set up your follow-up dates; and note any referrals you made or received during the interview. Use this tool as a place to log ideas or more success stories you can send to the interviewers. You can also go to *www.jibberjobber.com/blog* for ideas and suggestions from people who may have gone through interview and job search situations like yours.

Makini Theresa Harvey, CPRW, JCTC, CEIP, CCM

Career Abundance

Chapter 13

▶ **S**imple **T**ruths **A**bout
Thank-**Y**ou **L**etters

Whatever the results of your personal interview evaluation, following up with a thank-you letter to the interviewer(s) is essential. It's astonishing that only a very small percentage of candidates actually follow through on sending thank-you letters. Yet, this is understandable, as it's so easy to rationalize skipping this step—especially in the throes of an intensive job search. You're busy every moment, following up on leads from networking contacts, combing the Internet and other sources for job opportunities, and perhaps even juggling one or more jobs simultaneously—all while coping with the day-to-day barrage of family issues, economic pressures, and assorted other emergencies that invariably plague all of us. In the time-starved lives many of us lead, any corner that can be cut becomes fair game. This particular corner, though, is one that should not be cut!

Here are 10 simple truths about thank-you letters:

1. Sending thank-you letters to follow up on interviews is a vital step in the job-search process and can be decisive in winning job offers.

2. Thank-you letters yield returns on investment, both immediate and long-term, that are well worth your time and effort.

3. Send thank-you letters so that they arrive within 24 hours of your interview.

4. Highlight key points that you believe are important to reiterate or clarify, or bring to the interviewer's attention (if they did not surface during your interview).

5. Demonstrate that you have absorbed any information you learned about the organization during the interview.

6. If you met other key people while you were visiting the organization, be sure to mention their names.

7. Reconnect your skills and expertise to the organization's needs.

8. Express your enthusiasm about the opportunity.

9. Close with a call to action or by stating what your next step will be.

10. If you decide for any reason that you no longer wish to pursue the opportunity, write to thank the interviewer and withdraw yourself from consideration.

The value of sending thank-you letters to everyone you interviewed with is well worth your investment of time and effort—and even postage! I've worked with numerous clients who are convinced that their thank-you letters were crucial in setting them apart from other candidates. They believe they would not have received their job offers and, ultimately, the jobs they pursued without having sent these potentially tie-breaking letters. In fact, a number of candidates were later told by their employers that their prompt and compelling thank you letters were ultimately the decisive, distinguishing factors in choosing from among very strong and similarly qualified candidates.

It's vital to send thank-you letters immediately. For optimal effect, take steps to ensure they arrive in the recipients' hands within 24 hours of the interview, if at all possible. The target employer's timeline for filling the position is the key to determining your approach. If you believe that the hiring decision will be made imminently, then send an e-mail immediately following the interview. Follow it with a phone call within the next 24 to 48 hours, depending upon the target employer's stated schedule. Then send a letter, which can be a bit more extensive than the e-message, via overnight delivery.

Your interview experience should have provided you with some clues to the organizational culture, which will be helpful in deciding on the form that your thank-you communications should take. Remain mindful of time constraints imposed by the target employer's decision timeline. Faxing a conventional letter may be the most expedient option, depending on the circumstances and timing. Recognizing that it's dangerous to generalize, consider the following examples. It's often appropriate to send an e-mail to IT firms. By contrast, an exclusive, privately owned florist shop might warrant a handwritten note on elegant or quaint stationery or card, depending upon the nature of the shop. A conventional letter might be best for a community-based nonprofit organization. You might do well to send a uniquely designed, avant-garde, or classic card to an upscale, independent clothing store—again, depending on the type of merchandise and clientele. If you don't use fax or e-mail, and the recipient isn't local, it may be worth the cost and effort to send your communiqué via an overnight service to ensure next-day receipt.

Thank-you letters are important for all types of interviews, including in-person, telephone, video conference, and others. Be sure to make every effort to send some form of thanks to each and every person involved in the interview process. Mention the names of other people you met during your interview or tour of the organization. One of our clients sent 13 letters following an extensive process that involved two days of meetings with key stakeholders. She was pursuing a leadership position with a community-based nonprofit organization and had met with members of the board of directors and management staff, as well as government officials having agency oversight responsibility. It turned out that a couple of people scheduled to meet with her were suddenly unavailable. She sent letters to them, too. Each customized letter highlighted points of particular relevance to the stakeholder, and connected her qualifications directly to the organization's needs. The thank-you letters arrived the day after the last meeting, and she ultimately accepted their job offer.

There are three general categories of thank-you letters. After completing your interview self-evaluation, even if it's only a brief, initial assessment, it should be fairly clear which type of thank-you letter will serve your candidacy the most, and what its focus should be.

1. The pure thank-you. If you believe that you hit a home run and excelled beyond your wildest expectations, and that the interviewer was favorably impressed, then a simple expression of gratitude to the interviewer is adequate. Even if you feel highly confident, it's even more powerful to select a few key points mentioned during the interview as priorities for the position, and connect them to your qualifications. Be sure to include an enthusiastic reminder of why you are interested in working at that particular organization.

2. The reinforcer. This is to strengthen your candidacy if you believe any of the following are true: You could have more effectively related your competencies or experience to the needs of the organization, either voluntarily or in response to the interviewer's question(s); you didn't mention or adequately explain something that you believe is key to advancing your candidacy; or the interviewer was distracted by interruptions or appeared unfocused, and you wish to clearly state or reiterate key points that you believe were not adequately captured or fully understood by him or her.

3. The withdrawal. Another simple and universal truth is that it's best to leave doors open, or at least slightly ajar, whenever possible. A colleague's favorite saying is that a door is rarely closed without a window opening up somewhere else, often in a most unexpected place. So, even if you no longer wish to work at the organization, no matter the reason, it's a good idea to send a thank-you letter. Today's interviewer may be tomorrow's entrepreneur who may remember you years hence when he or she is seeking someone of your caliber. Or the interviewer may encounter another prospective employer seeking someone just like you tomorrow, or next week. If you have sent a cordial withdrawal letter, chances are much better that you'll be remembered with favor. Notice how networking operates all the time, in all situations. It may even turn out that whatever dissuaded you from pursuing the position will completely turn around in the near future. Suddenly, you may find yourself interested in pursuing an opportunity with this organization once again. If you leave on a sour note, your options will be much more limited than if you had behaved professionally and graciously.

Following are elements to be included in most thank-you letters, with examples.

▶ *Return address, inside address, date, and salutation:*

Zoe E. Mayberry
621 Lafayette Parkway
Penfield, New York 14526
555.555.9876
Jobseeker@localnet.net

August 1, 2008

Ms. Esmerelda Stevenson
Vice President, Human Resources
Enchanted Dolls of the World
1258 Village Green
Penfield, New York 14526

Dear Ms. Stevenson:

▶ *Friendly, cordial, and quick reminder of the interview (date, special circumstances, and so on):*

Thank you for the opportunity to interview for the Store Manager position at your satellite shop in the Medley Centre Mall yesterday.

▶ *Applying new information learned at the interview, briefly review key points made during the interview that are especially relevant to the target position:*

I appreciated your time, and very much enjoyed speaking with you about your plans for the new shoppe in Irondequoit, my hometown. It's delightful to be back after several years abroad, and to find that many of my regional contacts in the world of doll-making are still active in the field I love.

Especially in light of my strong interest and expertise in both bisque and soft-sculpture doll repair, I was thrilled to hear about your vision for the new doll hospital. I'm certain this will be a successful complement to doll sales. Your plans to begin offering selected antique dolls can only add to the appeal of this charming product line.

Reflecting on our conversation, I am even more convinced that my capabilities and experience seem tailor-made to excel in the role of store manager:

- Design and fabrication of one-of-a-kind dolls featured in *Doll Fancy Magazine* (January, 2001 and April, 2007 issues);

- Delicate, accurate repair of antique dolls using authentic, period materials.

▶ ***Close with a statement of your continuing enthusiasm and interest in the position, including a call to action or your planned follow-up:***

As a doll enthusiast with over twenty years of experience creating, repairing and promoting dolls as collectibles as well as meaningful toys, I am even more enthusiastic about this opportunity than when we first met. I look forward to continuing our dialog about ways my skills and abilities can contribute to the growth and success of your new venture, and hope to hear from you soon regarding the next step.

Sincerely,

Zoe E. Mayberry

Zoe E. Mayberry

A number of sample letters have been included on the following pages from each of the categories discussed. Feel free to let them inspire you to develop your own correspondence. The goal is for you to express yourself honestly and directly in your own words, in order to optimally advance your candidacy.

Tips From the Pros

You can move forward more rapidly in your job search by utilizing every opportunity to send a letter to a potential employer. Surprisingly, only a small percentage of candidates send a letter after an interview. A thank-you letter is an opportunity to show initiative, to emphasize a critical point about your background, to reflect personality and fit, and that may influence the hiring decision. Be sure to ask for a business card after an interview to check the spelling of names, and correct e-mail or snail mail address. The letter should be brief and if handwritten, legible.

Diane Irwin
Dynamic Résumés

The interview is over. Now what? Sending the interviewer(s) a professional, customized thank-you or follow-up letter within 24 hours of the meeting is critical for the job seeker who wants to stand out from the competition. Not only does this show continued interest in the role, but it also brings the candidate's name once again to the attention of the decision maker who will appreciate this professional courtesy of saying "Thanks for the opportunity!" [Here] is a sample of a follow-up letter that can be easily customized:

Dear Ms. <<Last Name>>,

Thank you for the opportunity to discuss your opening for a <<job posting title>>. I enjoyed meeting with you to learn more about <<company name>> and this intriguing career opportunity.

During our conversation, I was especially impressed with your organization's commitment to <<insert company attribute, mission, or accomplishment>> as this is also a passion of mine. My values and strong work ethic are a good fit for your organizational culture. I feel my career experience will complement and add value to your firm.

In our meeting, you also stressed the importance of <<job holder characteristics as indicated by the employer>> as critical elements for success in this role. Allow me to reiterate my talents to support my ability and desire to surpass your expectations:

- <<Insert relevant strength #1 from your resume>>
- <<Insert relevant strength #2 from your resume>>
- <<Insert relevant strength #3 from your resume>>

I hope that after our meeting you will agree that my extensive hands-on experience as a <<your current profession or title>> coupled with my educational background and training will be a great asset as your <<job posting title>>.

<<Company name>> will be the ideal organization to build on the career that I have established. I will be available immediately to begin work with your company.

Again, thank you for your time and I am looking forward to hearing from you soon.

Warm Regards,

Candice Candidate

Candice Candidate

Tanya Taylor, CHRP, CRS, TNT
Human Resources Management

Thank-you letters are *"second-tier" marketing communications.* They acknowledge the time and consideration of the hiring manager, thank him/her, and express your interest in the position. Don't stop selling your unique skills, qualifications, accomplishments, credentials and more. Relate how your experience is tied directly to the company's current challenges and needs. Share your past experiences in change management, reversing losses, delivering solid profit margins, successes in productivity and quality improvement, and all the other things you accomplished. Highlight how you solved similar problems to those of the hiring company. Share your past achievements in strengthening market position, expanding customer bases, and outperforming competitors. If the hiring company communicated an objection to hiring you, respond to it in the thank-you letter. If you forgot something really important about your experiences or qualifications during the interview, this is the tool to communicate those achievements, experiences, and qualifications. If there were no challenges, problems, objections and nothing that you forget to mention during the interview, then use the thank-you letter to further highlight your specific accomplishments. Thank-you letters don't have to be one-page long. Submit a powerful, well-worded, sales-directed, and competitive thank-you letter.

Doris Appelbaum, BA, MS

Appelbaum's Resume Professionals, Inc.

Sample Thank-You Letters

(Pure Thank-you)

MARK REYNALDO
81 Blind Bluff Circle • Rochester, New York 14688
585-972-3033
Reynaldo13@resumesos.com

June 12, 2008

Mr. Chip Circuit
Director of Product Development
Electronics Corporation
123 Technology Park
Rochester, New York 14699

Dear Mr. Circuit:

Thank you for taking the time to speak with me on Tuesday morning. I enjoyed meeting you and the other members of your team, and learning about your needs relevant to the Product Manager role we discussed.

Based on our conversation and my tour of your plant, I am convinced that Electronics Corporation offers a work environment and corporate culture in which I can both grow as a professional, and deliver significant value to your bottom line.

The needs assessment process you use to establish product features parallels the process we currently use at Analog Systems, and I believe I could quickly acclimate to your systems and procedures, allowing me to "hit the ground running."

I remain most interested in the position we talked about and in joining your team. Please contact me at your convenience to discuss next steps.

Thank you, again. I hope to further our conversations soon.

Sincerely yours,

Mark Reynaldo

Mark Reynaldo

(Pure Thank-You—Continuing Interest)

KELLIE ANN LEESON
3830 Pembroke Road
Clarence, New York 14033
716-698-4157

July 31, 2008

Ms. Katrina Yannick
Human Resources
Canisius College
2345 Main Street
Buffalo, New York 14299

Dear Ms. Yannick:

Thank you for taking the time to speak with me Friday morning. I really appreciated the opportunity to learn more about the Administrative Specialist position with your Alumni Affairs office. The opportunity to speak with Audra Vanderbilt, your Director of Development was most helpful in clarifying how effectively the two departments collaborate on exciting, college-wide initiatives. I share your enthusiasm surrounding the upcoming capital campaign; it's contagious!

As we discussed, the position calls for strong customer service skills and the ability to multi-task. Throughout my career, I have dealt with customers in a variety of circumstances, including often stressful situations. I've always been able to establish an excellent rapport with customers, resolve problems to maintain satisfaction and loyalty, and effectively address any other customer needs.

Currently, I am fulfilling the responsibilities of three people to meet the needs of my employer. In addition, I balance a variety of community activities, including leading a Camp Fire Girls group, coordinating scheduling for a recreational soccer league, and programming activities for a women's ministry at a local church. My success in achieving objectives in all these endeavors more than demonstrates the ability to multi-task.

I remain most interested in this position and look forward to continuing our conversations. I am confident that I can meet or exceed your expectations in this role. Please contact me to discuss next steps.

Thank you, again, for your time and interest.

Sincerely,

Kelly Ann Leeson

Kelly Ann Leeson

(Reinforcer—Connecting Strengths with Employer's Needs)

Paul Randall

2739 Oakcreek Circle
Irvine, CA 92618

Voice: 714/672-3269
Prandall@aol.com

June 10, 2008

Mr. Matt Spender
Vice President for Supply Chain Management
Manufacturing Industries, Inc.
1234 Industrial Parkway
Long Beach, CA 91827

Dear Mr. Spender:

First of all, thank you. I really enjoyed our conversation on June 9th and believe my knowledge, experience, and broad skill-set align well with your organization and would allow me to make meaningful contributions to its continued success. I am impressed with Manufacturing Industries' mission, goals, and strategies.

I am very interested and enthusiastic about becoming a part of your team as a Supply Chain Manager. Based on my successful career, I am confident I could bring extensive expertise to the position. Let me highlight what I consider to be my most valuable assets:

- *Knowledge* ... As you know, I possess an in-depth understanding of operations management, as well as a thorough comprehension of materials and distribution management acquired during my career in executive level positions in the consumer products industry.

- *Experience* ... As we discussed, my extensive business development and marketing management experience will prove to be beneficial to your organization. Additionally, my excellent leadership abilities and sales achievements exhibit my competence in areas key to surpassing expectations for the position.

- *Passion* ... I am ready, willing, and able to hit the ground running and would love to lead high producing teams and work collaboratively with your management group to increase revenues by utilizing my effective strategic planning and implementation abilities across multiple departments that built long-term value for corporations.

My profitable performance exhibits the significant benefits I can bring to Manufacturing Industries—today and in the future. You will also find that my talent to coach and motivate sales and manufacturing teams to attain higher goals, as well as my ability to cultivate and maintain business relationships with customers, national suppliers, and global vendors has always been the foundation for my success as confirmed by my ability to significantly expand market share.

I look forward to speaking with you again and would welcome further discussions regarding this opportunity that will definitely bring beneficial results to both of us. Again, thank you for your time and consideration. I wish you continued success in your business.

Sincerely,

Paul Randall

Paul Randall

- Pearl White, CPRW, JCTC, CEIP, A 1st Impression Resume Service

(Reinforcer—Reiterating Key Strengths)

Roslyn A. O'Brien

69 Village Green   Shaker Heights, Ohio 44099(216) 844-8079

June 24, 2008

Ms. Marie E. Hutchinson
Delaware State Librarian
P.O. Box 520
Dover, Delaware 19877-0520

Dear Marie:

Thank you for the opportunity to meet with you and the selection committee on Monday. I enjoyed our discussion of the Associate State Librarian opening. I was impressed with your vision for this individual's role.

Based on our conversation, I believe that I possess the capabilities to successfully meet your expectations for this key position with the State Library.

To reiterate the experiences I bring to this opportunity, please note the following:

- *Promoting programs and fostering working relationships with over 1,200 member libraries in all major segments of the field. These activities also encompass extensive community outreach.*

- *Providing strategic vision and mission, and motivating staff to pursue visionary goals. In two leadership assignments, I have recognized staff for their efforts and given them the guidance and direction that has delivered exceptional program results.*

- *Managing capital projects and spearheading information technology initiatives. These encompassed upgrades to comply with ADA access requirements, renovations that improved space utilization, and leading efforts to incorporate technology into library settings.*

- *Supervising departments in urban and suburban settings to address a broad range of competing priorities. Among these experiences was the supervision of an Interlibrary Loan department serving 127 individual branches in a seven-county area.*

I am most interested in this position and am confident that my track record demonstrates my capacity to "hit the ground running," and apply my leadership, enthusiasm, and expertise to furthering the mission of Delaware libraries in this key role. I look forward to continuing our discussions in the near future.

Sincerely,

Roslyn A. O'Brien

Roslyn A. O'Brien

(Reinforcer—Recovering From Interview Disaster)

Carla A. Nottingham

669 Lakeside Village   Franklin Lakes, New Jersey 07899   (201) 844-8979

June 15, 2008

Ms. Kirsten Dailey
Director of Branch Libraries
Philadelphia Public Library
1455 Franklin Boulevard
Philadelphia, Pennsylvania 19199-1234

Dear Ms. Dailey:

Thank you for the opportunity to discuss the position of Associate Director for Branch Libraries with you at the ALA Spring Conference. I was sorry that you were called away so suddenly, and hope that the family crisis you alluded to was favorably resolved.

In the brief time we had together, I was impressed with your outline of the position and have reviewed the materials you left with me. I am convinced that I possess the capabilities to be successful in this role.

Some of my key areas of expertise that your time constraints did not permit us to discuss in depth include:

- *Dynamic leadership that included establishing a strategic vision and motivating staff to pursue that vision.* It is essential to ensure that consideration of new or expanded services is done within the context of the strategic framework: vision, mission, and strategic plan. Continuous monitoring and rigorous evaluation of current programs are vital components of this process. When I assumed the Directorship of the Northeast Keystone Library Cooperative (NKLC), one of the first steps I took was to eliminate obsolete and underused programs.

- *Successfully managing change while creating a positive work environment where employees feel empowered.* As Director of the Appaloosa Free Library, I recognized that the culture of the organization needed a shift. Even in light of the budget constraints and facilities' physical limitations, the library provided good service. However, staff and trustees' hope and optimism had been eroded over years of failure to achieve increased funding prior to my tenure. Within two years, I was able to shift the paradigm that led to modernization of programs, services, and infrastructure.

- *Developing information technology plans that have prepared libraries for the 21st century and that anticipate the changing technological landscape, and implementation of these plans even in the face of resistance.* When I began at the Appaloosa Free Library (1992), there was one PC in the entire facility. The former director had taken a public stand against automation, and a great deal of finesse was needed to persuade funding bodies that additional resources should be allocated to this area. I began work on a three-year technology plan, which included development of a LAN to allow the branch libraries to network. The position of Computer Librarian was established and staff began training patrons on the Internet. The program was successful, and we were the first library in the county to have a website.

I am confident that my knowledge and expertise would allow me to exceed your expectations in this leadership role and look forward to further discussing my candidacy with you soon.

Sincerely,

C. A. Nottingham
Carla A. Nottingham

(Handwritten Thank-You Note)

July 12, 2008

Dear Shannon,

Thanks so much for taking time to speak with me on Monday. I enjoyed meeting you and your staff and am much impressed with the wonderful products you sell at Handbags & More. In fact, I'm coming back this weekend with my Mom and sister to shop for new canvas tote bags.

Based on our conversation, I believe that managing your new Eastview Mall location would be a great career move for me, and I would enjoy working with other members of your team to make the new store a success. I hope we can talk again soon about this great opportunity!

Yours truly,

Veronica

(Thank-You E-mail Message)

To: chip.circuit@anaologsolutions.com

Cc: tom.transitor@analogsolutions.com; wally.firewall@analogsolutions.com; Polly.personnel@analogsolutions.com

Subject: Follow-Up to Today's Meeting

Chip & Everyone,

Great meeting all of you today and learning about the spectacular things you're doing at Analog.

Would really love to join your team and believe that my Software Engineering, Project Management, and Product Development experience could be a huge asset on the "Moonwalk" program we discussed.

Hope to chat again soon. Feel free to call my cell (585-987-6543) or reach me at this e-mail address.

Best regards,

Java Applet

(Withdrawing While Keeping the Door Open)

Christine Livingston

1819 Penfield Road   Penfield, New York 14526   (585) 377-9876

August 26, 2008

Mr. William Thomas
CEO
Manchester Software, LLC
4310 Magnolia Street
Shortsville, New York 14599

Dear Mr. Thomas:

Thank you for taking the time to meet with me recently to discuss the Director of Product Development position. I genuinely appreciated the opportunity to meet with your team and to learn about the position.

Although I was impressed with your firm and the potential for this opportunity, I have decided to continue searching for a position which more closely mirrors my long-range career goals. For this reason, I must ask that my name be withdrawn from further consideration for the Director of Product Development role.

I wish you the best of luck in your search and am confident that you will find the right person for the job from among the many qualified candidates who have applied.

Thank you, again, for your time and consideration.

Sincerely yours,

Christine Livingston

Christine Livingston

Chapter 14

▶ Simple Truths About Following Up to Close the Deal

So you've prepared for the interview, gone to the interview and performed well, sent your thank-you letter immediately after the interview, and are now sitting back waiting for that job offer you just know is coming any day now. Not so fast! If you were the first of many candidates interviewed, or some corporate crisis has totally distracted the decision-maker(s) from the hiring process, the interviewer may have forgotten about you. Sure, it's hard to believe (because you know you're the best candidate for the job), but such things can happen.

In order to keep your candidacy alive and well, to emerge as the top candidate, and to achieve your ultimate goal of getting hired, keep these truths in mind:

1. Become part of the hiring process.
2. Timeline and culture are key.
3. Strive to stay alive and remain top-of-mind.
4. What goes around really does come around.
5. Keep your references in the loop.
6. Get organized and keep track of your progress.

Simple Truth #1:
Become Part of the Hiring Process

Once you've sent your initial thank-you communication, it's time to move forward to the next phase of your follow-up. Since your appointment, the interviewer may have met with numerous other candidates. As difficult as this may be to accept, you may no longer be top-of-mind. Furthermore, during the course of these discussions with other candidates, new issues or concerns may have been raised that the interviewer didn't consider when talking with you. Depending on how long the hiring process actually takes, the target employer may now be contemplating new tasks and/or challenges that the new employee will be faced with, and which never came up during your interview. Because neither of you were aware of these expectations for the position, perhaps you never fully demonstrated your capabilities in these areas. By taking an active approach to following up, you can actually become part of the hiring process, rather than passively waiting...and waiting some more, while subsequent candidates gain an advantage.

Simple Truth #2:
Timeline and Culture Are Key

Develop the most effective format and timing for your follow-up based on the target employer's decision-making schedule and the corporate culture. Strike a healthy balance between keeping your image fresh in the interviewer's mind and not becoming a nuisance. Your approach will necessarily differ among various types of prospective employers. Pick up on cues about what the preferred method of contact is for each employer, and carefully record what the interviewer divulges about the hiring timeline. For example, if the interviewer has indicated that the hiring decision will be made within the week, your follow-up will be somewhat compressed. The hiring process often takes much longer than prospective employers anticipate, but it's still important to be mindful of their stated goals and plan accordingly.

Simple Truth #3: Strive to Stay Alive and Remain Top-of-Mind

The simple truth is that after the interview, if you haven't yet received an offer and still wish to pursue the target position, your objective is to keep your name in front of the interviewer without becoming a nuisance. It's vital to be top-of-mind while the hiring authorities work through their decision-making process.

Your initial thank-you to the interviewer serves several purposes. First, it expresses your genuine gratitude for the opportunity, and for the interviewer having squeezed you into what's likely a very full schedule. Second, it clarifies any points needing clarification, and fills in any blanks that struck you as needing to be filled in. Third, it continues the "conversation" that began with your initial cover letter and was carried through into the interview.

The follow-up phone call

Most job-search experts agree that, in general, it's best to wait no more than five days from the date of your interview to place a follow-up phone call—that is, unless the interviewer specifically asks that you not call at all, or unless you have other instructions from the target employer. The interviewer should have already received your thank-you letter (or card or e-mail) by now, and this is your opportunity to take another step in continuing the dialogue.

It's absolutely vital that you prepare carefully for this phone call. A simple, "So, how's the search going?" is wholly inadequate. It's unprofessional and, worst of all, doesn't ask for the precise information that will help you stay in the running. Be prepared to leave a voicemail message. Be sure to have your notes in front of you, and make sure you're in a quiet place without likely interruptions. (You may wish to review the section on telephone interviews in Chapter 6.) You will be making another impression on the interviewer that can either help you ace the situation or destroy your chances of getting a job offer.

After you have identified yourself and reminded the interviewer of the position you're pursuing, consider opening with something similar to this: "As you move through the search process and interview other candidates, I imagine the requirements of the position may be evolving—are you still looking for the skills we discussed in our meeting last Wednesday? Or have your expectations for the position changed at all?" This is a subtle way of letting the interviewer know that you're a savvy pro who understands the dynamics of hiring the best. This approach also gives the interviewer a chance to acknowledge that the target employer's needs for the position may have shifted. Notice how you're continuing the dialogue—again, by making a connection with the interviewer, and by expressing that you recognize the dynamics of the process.

Remember to have your resume and success stories spread out in front of you as you make this phone call, and be prepared to think on your feet. If the interviewer admits that, yes, there are some new expectations that have cropped up for the position, you had better be prepared to demonstrate that it's just fine by you. In fact, you're *excited* or *thrilled* to hear about these new requirements because you realize that you didn't have a chance to talk much about your experience in one of your previous jobs, in which you were accountable for [insert the new area(s) identified by the interviewer]: "You'll note on my resume that not only did I streamline the process for efficiently disseminating new information on existing products to our sales force, but I was a key contributor to reducing costs for sales collaterals by more than 15 percent."

Before the phone call concludes, be sure to ask if there is any other information you could provide that would be helpful. Then you may inquire about the timeline:

"When do you think you'll be making a decision?" Depending upon the tone of the discussion up to this point, you may also consider asking, "When may I check back with you?" Be guided by the interviewer's responses in planning your next steps. Depending upon the timeline stated, calling once a week may be appropriate. If the hiring horizon is longer, perhaps once every two or three weeks would be best.

Thoughts on reaching the interviewer

In many organizations, voice mail has replaced the receptionist or executive secretary as the ultimate gatekeeper, fostering or hindering direct contact with the interviewer. It's impossible to overstate the importance of being prepared with a smooth, coherent message should you encounter voice mail. You may consider experimenting with calling early or late in the day, on the theory that things may become busier during the middle of the day. Some experts recommend placing follow-up calls before the official start of the business day or after 5 p.m. Others contend that busy decision-makers who are on the job that early or late would not be pleased at the prospect of having their "quiet time" interrupted. Again, learning as much as possible about the culture and timeline is your best bet to help ensure direct contact. Just as you were prepared for incoming phone calls starting from the moment you sent out your first cover letter and resume, be sure that everyone in your household remains on alert for such calls if you leave a follow-up message.

If the interviewer has stated flatly that follow-up phone calls would not be welcome, consider sending a letter or e-mail in one of two different forms:

1. The nudge. Your initial follow-up letter (the letter that follows your thank-you letter) should focus on these simple truths: You're still enthusiastic about the job and want it; you understood the information shared during the interview; and, based on that understanding, you're even more convinced that your unique value would significantly contribute to the target employer's mission and its success. In subsequent letters, consider including a news clipping that's especially relevant to the industry or job, or even a thought-provoking, tasteful cartoon.

2. The non-rejection. If you are notified that another candidate has been selected for the position that you were pursuing, you have a terrific opening to demonstrate yet again that you're gracious, professional, and still interested in other opportunities with the organization. Sending a letter at this time will definitely set you apart from the average job seeker, and most interviewers will appreciate and remember the gesture.

Simple Truth #4:
What Goes Around Really Does Come Around

Maintain your enthusiastic attitude and professional, gracious demeanor in absolutely all communications, written or verbal, with the representatives of the target employer. It's impossible to predict when you might encounter the same interviewer in completely different circumstances, when parting on a pleasant note might make a tremendous difference in how things proceed. In this age of Internet networking (using FaceBook, MySpace, and so on), it's also quite possible that your interviewer may be acquainted with others who have influence over your future job prospects. Behaving in a professional, cordial manner pays dividends well into future years. There's also a possibility that the other candidate who was hired for your target position might not work out and the position may be open again six months (or even as soon as six weeks) down the road, in which case you'll want the interviewer(s) to remember you favorably.

Simple Truth #5:
Keep Your References in the Loop

What your references say about your skills and strengths may be even more compelling for the interviewer than what you say about yourself. Be sure to apprise your references of your status throughout the process. Check in with them and let them know that you have just interviewed with a company. Fill them in on highlights of your discussion with the interviewer, and, if necessary, remind them how your experience meshes with the expectations of the target position. Identify several specifics for them. You may even offer to e-mail or fax them a summary for their reference. Be sure to reiterate your thanks for their help and support. Then, later in the process, find out what the interviewer asked your references. Do there seem to be any areas of your background or capabilities that trouble the prospective employer? If so, when you follow up again with the interviewer, find a way to subtly address these areas and overcome any objections that may have cropped up.

Simple Truth #6:
Get Organized and Keep Track of
Your Progress

Establish good record-keeping procedures to be able to stay on top of multiple opportunities at once and know when you're due to take the next step in each of your follow-up plans.

Presumably you have some sense of the hiring timeline by the end of each interview. Keep careful records of your contacts with prospective employers, including the interviewer's schedule for filling the position. Job seekers have discovered some popular online resources for keeping track of job-search information (some of these are listed in Appendix C). If you prefer a more traditional approach, set up a simple spreadsheet to track all of your job leads, either electronically (for example, in Microsoft's Excel) or on paper (see Appendix B). If you find yourself pursuing more than one target position at a time (and hopefully you will), it's easy to lose track of where you are in the process with each employer. Solid record-keeping habits will make it easier to monitor progress with a number of leads simultaneously.

Once you have initiated a record-keeping system that suits you, be sure to keep on top of what's happening, or not happening, as the case may be. It's too easy to passively drift along, waiting for the next phone call or e-mail from the prospective employer. To continue to distinguish yourself from the crowd of candidates, it's vital to proactively follow up on your interviews. Remember that in today's job market, employers are looking for candidates with a little something extra—motivation, perseverance, composure under pressure, breadth or depth of experience—and your ability to follow up in a professional manner can go a long way toward distinguishing you from the crowd of other candidates.

Tips From the Pros

After an interview, many job hunters never hear from the company again. This is often (correctly) perceived as rejection. Getting rejected for a position can deflate your enthusiasm, especially if you really wanted the job. When you believe you built rapport with others and had the qualifications for the position it is hard to let go and move on. Tony, a business major, still employs an academic approach to interviewing. When he is rejected for a position he thought he had a good chance of getting (or doesn't hear back from them), he calls the person he interviewed with and asks for constructive feedback. "I have gotten some excellent feedback on my resume, how I present myself, and what kind of experience I am lacking in getting the kind of job I want. Sure it's hard, but I pretend I am doing research on someone else so I don't take the criticism personally." The key is to find a way to depersonalize the rejection and keep multiple irons in the fire so your hopes won't be dashed when one single job falls through.

Gail Frank, NCRW, CPRW, JCTC, CEIP, MA

Employment University

Sample Follow-Up Letters

("Nudge" Follow-Up Letter)

Angela BelGeddes
68 Crystal Valley Crescent
Ontario, New York 14519
Angela.BelGeddes@Yahoo.com
315.886.9173

January 13, 2008

Trevor L. Wallingford, CPA
Wallingford, Pinkerton and Parsons, LLC
600 Midtown Tower, Suite 620
Rochester, New York 14604

Dear Mr. Wallingford:

I'm writing to express my continuing enthusiasm for the position of Junior Auditor with your firm. Reflecting on our first meeting on January 6, I realize that we focused on my technical training, experience, and abilities in some depth. I also want to let you know that I am very enthusiastic about the prospect of joining your team. Both John Pinkerton and Molly Parsons impressed me as hardworking and dedicated to the highest ethical standards and performance expectations.

Aware that you and your staff face tight deadlines, particularly at this time of year, I want to emphasize my proven track record as a quick study who is highly motivated to learn independently, as necessary.

Thank you again for the opportunity to learn more about your firm. I look forward to hearing from you soon. If you have any additional questions for me, please feel free to contact me at your earliest convenience.

Very truly yours,

Angela BelGeddes

Angela BelGeddes

("Second Nudge" Follow-Up Letter)

Angela BelGeddes
68 Crystal Valley Crescent
Ontario, New York 14519
Angela.BelGeddes@Yahoo.com
315.886.9173

January 21, 2008

Trevor L. Wallingford, CPA
Wallingford, Pinkerton and Parsons, LLC
600 Midtown Tower, Suite 620
Rochester, New York 14604

Dear Mr. Wallingford:

Thank you again for the opportunity to interview for the position of Junior Auditor with your firm. I remain enthusiastic at the prospect of joining your team and meeting the needs of your clients in the areas of audit and tax preparation.

While I realize that this is an extremely intense season for you, I simply could not resist sharing the enclosed ironically humorous cartoon highlighting the challenges faced by small entities striving to comply with the Sarbannes-Oxley requirements.

Upon reflection, I am even more convinced that my skills, capabilities, and natural aptitude could add value to your team of professionals. Please feel free to contact me at your convenience if there is any further information I could provide to assist in your hiring decision. In the meantime, I plan to phone you early next week to further our dialogue.

Thank you.

Very truly yours,

Angela BelGeddes

Angela BelGeddes

Enclosure: Cartoon re. Sarbannes-Oxley

(Revive/Rekindle Interest)

Miranda Ortega-Joseph

268 Hibiscus Court
Rochester, New York 14608
585.288.6901 Miranda.Jo@gmail.com

September 13, 2008

Lillian Sepulveda, D. Ed., Director
Association of Child Care Providers
7829 East Henrietta Road
Rush, New York 14543

Dear Dr. Sepulveda:

It's been several weeks since I had the privilege of meeting with you and members of your staff at your new headquarters in Rush. My understanding is that you will be reaching a decision soon about the new Program Director position, and you'll likely wish to select someone who shares your vision for new and expanded program offerings, who supports you in your initiatives, and who values teamwork.

My reputation for innovation across a broad range of classroom settings, and designing customized curricula to meet the needs of students from different backgrounds is a point of pride for me. In addition, providing strong leadership as a team leader is something to which I am deeply committed.

It is my sincere hope that as you move forward in your decision-making process that you will continue to consider my candidacy. I would be thrilled to join your staff in this key role and feel that I would be able to advance ACCP's mission in the Greater Rochester community.

Please feel free to contact me if there's any additional information you need regarding my credentials and / or professional accomplishments.

Thank for your time. I look forward to an opportunity to speak with you further.

Sincerely,

Miranda Ortega-Joseph

Miranda Ortega-Joseph

(Follow-Up After Rejection Letter—Stating Continuing Interest)

DARREN PARKHURST
777 Maplewood Terrace
Binghamton, New York 13946
607-851-6144

July 31, 2008

Hon. John A. Williams, Mayor
City of Endicott
City Hall, Room 73-B
Endicott, New York 13708-0001

Dear Mayor Williams:

Thank you for the opportunity to interview for the Neighborhood Office for Community Action (NOCA) Director position. I genuinely appreciated the chance to discuss your vision for the NOCA program.

Although another candidate was ultimately selected for this important position, I was pleased to be among the short list of applicants under final consideration.

As we have discussed, I believe that my 12 years of experience with the City of Binghamton provides me with a wealth of knowledge and expertise that can be beneficial to your municipality. I continue to be committed to the mission of the NOCA Program, but also wish to offer myself as a candidate for other roles where my capabilities can further the objectives of the City.

To briefly reiterate, some of the qualities that I can bring to a new position include:

- **Strategic vision, creative energy, and strong leadership skills.**

- **Capacity to build collaborative teams across public and private sectors.**

- **Excellent project management capabilities.**

- **Ability to build employee morale and inspire team members to strive for excellence.**

- **Innovative problem-solving skills.**

Please keep me in mind if other opportunities should arise where my talents would be an asset, particularly as you move ahead with implementation of *Endicott Plan 21.* I would enjoy speaking with you further to discuss how I can best serve your City's needs.

Thank you, again, for your consideration.

Sincerely,

D. Parkhurst

Darren Parkhurst

Chapter 15

▶ Simple Truths About
Subsequent Interviews

You've done everything right so far. You developed a winning resume and cover letter (with the help of *No-Nonsense Resumes* and *No-Nonsense Cover Letters*, of course!), and successfully identified and marketed yourself to target employers. You thoroughly prepared and put your best foot forward at the initial interview, and you followed up promptly, remaining mindful of the interviewer's preferences, the corporate culture, and the hiring timeline.

Then it happens: The phone rings! It's the interviewer's assistant, and you can feel your heart begin to race as you anticipate an imminent job offer. You expect the interviewer to come on the line at any moment, but instead, the assistant matter-of-factly informs you that you have been selected to come back for a second interview. *What?* Sometimes, you'll even receive a letter or e-mail advising you that at some future point, you will be invited in for a second meeting. In some instances, most often in connection with government jobs, you'll receive a letter or postcard with the date and time of your already scheduled next appointment.

The fact that you've been invited back for a second interview definitely improves your odds of receiving a job offer. You've cleared a hurdle and made it to the next step in the process. Congratulations—this is great news! However, this also means it's time to get back to work.

As with any competitive situation, the further up the ladder you climb in pursuit of your goal, the more rigorous the competition becomes. Like you, your remaining rivals for the target position are the best of the best, having cleared the same hurdles to make it to the next round. As you get yourself ready for this semifinal round, consider these important truths:

- ▶ All of the logistical guidelines for initial interviews (for example, grooming, wardrobe, punctuality, and demeanor) still apply.

- ▶ When you're invited for the next interview, be sure to ask if there is anything specific you should prepare or bring.

- ▶ Expect a different style of interview in subsequent meetings; you may even be asked to take a test or two.

- ▶ It's appropriate and even expected at this stage to ask deeper, more detailed questions based on everything you have learned thus far.

- ▶ Identify and close any gaps between the target employer's needs and what you can deliver.

- ▶ Be prepared to discuss compensation, but let the interviewer introduce the subject.

- ▶ Demonstrate your desire for the position—ask for the job!

- ▶ Remember to take names; request business cards from everyone you meet.

- ▶ Stay in touch even if you aren't chosen for the job.

It's not unusual to be called back for more than one follow-up interview. Generally, this indicates that there are several equally qualified candidates, and the interviewer/ employer is highly motivated and determined to select the candidate who will best fulfill the needs of the position while also being the best "fit," now and in the foreseeable future. Hiring a new employee represents a significant investment on the employer's part, one that goes well beyond the salary number. In addition to other costs such as medical benefits, mandated insurances, training, and the like, a hiring mistake costs an employer dearly in one of its most precious assets: opportunity cost, or time.

Simple Truth #1:
Prepare, Prepare, Prepare!

Use the information you learned at the first interview to beef up your preparation for a second interview. For example, perhaps you wore a suit, and you noticed that everyone else was dressed significantly more casually than you. For the next meeting, be sure your attire is still clean, tidy, and flawless (no jeans with holes or rips!), even if the interviewer invited you to dress more casually.

Redouble your efforts prior to your next interview to learn even more about the target employer. If you're not successful in your independent Internet-based research, feel free to ask for help from the chamber of commerce or public library. Depending on the nature of the meeting, you may want to bring along current press clippings, as there may be opportunities to discuss these current issues or events.

Brush up on your success stories, especially in connection with any new information you've learned about the position. Practice once again with a friend, focusing on questions that you still find especially challenging.

Simple Truth #2:
Follow the Interviewer's Instructions

When you ask if there is anything in particular you should bring to the next meeting, follow through with any instructions you're given! Depending on your field, this could be anything from elements of your professional portfolio, to other examples of your work, to letters of recommendation from prior employers, to a Number-2 pencil for use in taking a standardized test.

Simple Truth #3:
Expect a Different Interview Style

If your first interview consisted primarily of sitting in a room with a single interviewer, chances are that your next interview will be significantly different. You may be introduced to members of the department in which you would be working. If the initial interviewer was not the manager or direct supervisor of the target position, you may be introduced to and/or interviewed at length by that person. Sometimes, the second meeting is used as an opportunity for a number of key stakeholders to get to know you in a variation of the panel interview. The options are fairly open-ended. If you were initially interviewed by a panel, your next interview may be more in-depth, with just one or two people. Again, the target employer's goal is to do everything possible to ensure that you're the right fit for the position and the organization. Help them see that you are!

Simple Truth #4:
Ask More Questions

To prepare for subsequent interviews, gather and synthesize everything you have learned thus far, including information gleaned from earlier interview(s), from feedback reported by your references, and from your research on the target employer. In general, the more senior the position, the more questions you can and should ask. It's more appropriate to ask deeper, more detailed questions in subsequent interviews with managers, as opposed to those with HR representatives.

Asking your questions also lets you demonstrate that you have done your homework. For example, "I read in the current issue of [*Relevant Trade Journal*] that a company in Canada experimented with this approach to the issue. What are your thoughts on that?"

Subsequent interviews present you with an opportunity to invite the interviewer to disclose an opinion about you, and to ultimately agree that you are a strong candidate. At an appropriate point during your discussion, try saying something like this: "I've enjoyed hearing more about the organization and the position. My understanding is that you need someone who can [key skill] to achieve [successful result, however it is measured]. We've discussed my skills and experience, and I am confident I would bring key value to this role and would make a solid contribution here. From your point of view, what do you think is my greatest asset vis-à-vis this position?"

Depending on how much time has elapsed since the last meeting, some of the following questions may be appropriate. If the initial interviewer is not participating in the meeting, then adapt the questions accordingly:

▶ Has the position description changed since we last spoke?

▶ Are you still looking for the same skills and experience as when we met last month?

▶ Are there any new issues that I may address at this point?

Simple Truth #5:
Identify and Close Any Gaps

During the initial interviews, identify any gaps between what the target employer needs and what you said you will bring to the position. Again, consider feedback from your references: Were there any hot-button issues that came up during their conversations? Did the interviewer indicate any particular areas of concern about your qualifications or capabilities?

Based on everything you now know, carefully consider whether the position and employer would be a good fit for you. Then, if you truly believe that you have what it takes to succeed in the position, develop or dust off success stories that clearly show you are capable of doing whatever it takes to achieve the employer's objectives. No matter what kind of interview the next one is, find a way to work these stories into the discussion.

Simple Truth #6:
Let the Interviewer Introduce the Subject of Compensation

During a second interview, you may be tempted to inquire about salary and benefits. It's highly recommended that you not discuss compensation at all unless and until there is an offer on the table. If you do receive a job offer, it's important that you not feel pressured to commit to an answer on the spot. In general, it's best to ask for time to consider the offer properly; you don't want to seem too eager—plus, this is a major decision that requires your best energy and genuine reflection before responding. Most companies do not insist on an instant answer, so sincerely thank the interviewer and ask for some time to review the offer. If they do insist on knowing your answer right away, unless there are extenuating circumstance, think carefully about possible reasons for the pressure; perhaps there is a problem that has not been disclosed to you that would alter your opinion of the employer.

Simple Truth #7:
Ask for the Job!

My professional colleagues—search experts all—frequently relate anecdotes from disappointed or frustrated hiring managers that boil down to this: The candidate interviewed well, but he/she never asked for the job! After all, this is the ultimate demonstration of your enthusiasm, confidence, and genuine interest in the position.

If you truly believe that you would add value to the organization and have what it takes to succeed in the position, consider adapting the following to your own unique circumstances: "You won't find anyone who brings more commitment or enthusiasm for their work to this position. I'm confident I can exceed your expectations. If you present a reasonable offer today, I'd be delighted to join your team tomorrow."

Simple Truth #8:
Take Names and Gather Information

Your diligent follow-up should include making sure that you have contact information for everyone you meet during subsequent interviews. Ask everyone you speak with for their business card, and think about offering them your own (even if it's something you printed yourself on your home computer). Thank-you letters, notes, and/or e-mails are in order for everyone involved. Even if you walk out of the interview with a job offer in hand, be sure to send them to everyone you spoke with, from the CEO to the receptionist. If you land the job, you're starting off on the right foot with your new colleagues. If there are going to be additional rounds of interviews, you've put your name in front of the key people one more time, helping you to stay top-of-mind. If one of your competitors fails to send thank-yous, you've just differentiated yourself. If you skipped over Chapter 13, now's a good time to go back and review it.

In addition, everything mentioned in Chapter 14 about following up doubly applies now that you've had a second interview. If you don't close the deal and walk out of the second interview with a job offer in hand, be sure to do the following:

> Ask the interviewer what the decision-making timeline is. Try to get him or her to give you a specific date when the final hiring decision will be made.

> If the employer raised any concerns, no matter how small, about your qualifications, address them in a follow-up letter that relates your experiences to that area of qualification, or at least reiterate what a quick study you are and/or offer to undertake the necessary training to meet their particular need.

> Keeping the timeline in mind, stay in touch with the employer, either through the HR representative or by talking directly to the hiring decision-maker, to make sure that deadline doesn't pass without your receiving the employer's full consideration.

> If the deadline passes and you're certain no one has been chosen for the position, don't become discouraged. Make it your routine to call your contacts within the company at least once a week for an update. At some point they may tell you that hiring for this position is on hold or postponed. Ask them frankly when they believe the process will move forward; depending on their answer, continue to stay in touch (though perhaps not so frequently) in order to stay in the loop and avoid getting passed over.

Simple Truth #9:
Stay in Touch Even if You Aren't Chosen for the Job

Once you learn that another candidate has been selected, it's very easy, even human nature, to just walk away and forget about this missed opportunity. If you made it to a second or third interview, you must have impressed someone, and that someone may be pleased to help you in the future. An interviewer may even feel a little guilty that he or she didn't hire you, or you may have been someone's first choice, but that someone was outvoted by other decision-makers.

A savvy job seeker will recognize that this is still a golden opportunity to network with people who can help advance your career. One of the people who interviewed you may know someone else who has a similar opening, or, at the very least, may know which companies are hiring. In an organization that is in flux, additional openings may come up sooner than anticipated, and if you're still top-of-mind with the key contacts at that company, you may be the first one contacted about any new opportunities.

Therefore, it's wise to stay in touch with those you meet during your job search and make them part of your professional network. Be sure to pass along your own business cards, as well. Who knows? You may one day be in a position to recommend one of them for a position with the company that ultimately hires you, a scenario that can be "win-win-win" for everyone.

Tips From the Pros

Show Your Value

Second interviews are often difficult for employers because everyone they are evaluating is qualified. How can you set yourself apart as the best candidate? Let the employer see that you can make an immediate impact. Present potential employers with a sales/action plan that outlines your goals for a set period of time: 30, 60, 90 days or 3, 6, 9, 12 months. The plan should be one sheet, and it should state realistic goals that can be measured. For example:

First 30 days

- Develop thorough knowledge of products

- Meet key vendors

- Shadow experienced sales reps on presentations

First 60 days

- Contact 100 prospects

- Lead 35 sales presentations

- Work with Sales Manager to prepare bids and contracts

First 90 days

- Close 15 sales

- Follow up with lukewarm prospects

- Initiate 50-75 new contacts

Employers hire candidates who make them confident. Presenting a sales/action plan shows that you are focused, independent, and success-oriented. Who would not want to hire such a person?

Clay Cerny

AAA Targeted Writing & Coaching

Good news! You've done well in your first interview, and the employer has invited you back for a second interview. Will it be different from the first interview? What should you expect? How should you prepare? Here's a list to help you do well in the second interview.

- Research the company, the industry, and the competitors. Assuming you did your research before the first interview, dig a little deeper to learn more about the company's challenges and how you can address them.

- If your second interview is at a different venue than your first (perhaps your first interview was on the phone?), make sure you know how to get to the interview and arrive at least 15 minutes early.

- Pay particular attention to your wardrobe and grooming, taking into account the style and culture of the company, as you perceived it at the first interview.

- Ask questions at the interview. Focus on the company's plans for the future and your career prospects.

- Answer questions your interviewers ask, honestly and succinctly. There may be people present who are not aware that you have been asked the same questions before.

- Leave all discussions of salary until you are offered the job, unless the company broaches the subject. (See Chapter 11 for specific advice on salary discussions.)

- If you feel positive about the job, ask for it!

- Be prepared to accept the job if it's offered.

Deanne Arnath, CPRW

A Resume Wizard & Services

If you have been asked to return for a second or even third interview, you have obviously done something right while interviewing. To keep the momentum going you must prepare additionally for the next interview phase. Study your comments and reviews from the first interview to find out what they are still looking for. Use this information to research additional company information. Review your own experience to uncover additional examples of the skills you are trying to convey. On the interview day, know where you are going, who you will be interviewing with, and their title and job descriptions. Dress appropriately, take the necessary items for the interview, and bring healthy snacks for added energy in case it is a long day. Readdress any unanswered or unclear questions left over from the first interview and any new questions you may have. This interviewer may be looking at your behavioral patterns, how well you will fit within the department and company, and what potential contributions you can offer to the company. It is, therefore, very important to be friendly, work to match your behavior and energy level with the interviewer's, and determine if this company feels like the right fit for you.

Kris Plantrich, CPRW, CEIP

ResumeWonders Writing and Career Coaching Services

Appendix A

▶ Interview Take-Alongs

Use this checklist to spark your own ideas about what to bring to the interview:

☑ **Resume.** Take at least 10 copies. You may need to hand them out to others you meet, and it's easier if you have them with you rather than the interviewer potentially scrambling at the last minute to have copies made—or retrieved from having been misplaced. Being prepared in this way also demonstrates your ability to plan ahead, and further shows your genuine interest in the position.

☑ **Cover letter** if you sent one originally. In case any questions come up, it's helpful to have a copy.

☑ **Reference sheet.**

☑ **Position description/job posting,** if applicable.

☑ **Portfolio of accomplishments,** depending on your field.

☑ **Organized compilation of your research on the target employer.**

☑ **List of questions you wish to ask the interviewer.**

☑ **Business cards.** If you don't have business cards from your current job, or prefer not to hand them out during your job search, have some professionally printed or use one of the many easy-to-use computer programs to create your own.

☑ **Note pad and two pens.**

☑ **Specific requests the interviewer may have made,** such as performance appraisals, letters of recommendation, school transcripts, and the like.

☑ **Single briefcase** or neat folder to accommodate your documents. It presents a more polished image if you have your materials neatly organized in one place instead of multiple tote bags, handbags, or no bag at all. Be sure that your case includes only materials relevant for the interview at hand. (Under the pressure of an interview, it's too easy to quickly grab and pull out a document that you're certain is your reference sheet, for example, only to have it turn out to be a handout from a previous interview.)

☑ **Map/directions.**

☑ **Automobile club membership card** with emergency contact number.

☑ **Cell phone** (be sure to turn it off when you arrive!).

☑ **Extra cash** (small bills and loose change for cab fare, parking meters, parking garages, restaurant tips, and so on).

☑ **Small comb or brush** for last-minute primping.

☑ **Lip balm.**

☑ **Small mirror** in case one isn't readily available in the restroom (it happens!).

☑ **Breath mints** or dissolving breath-freshening sheets.

☑ **Facial tissues.**

Appendix B

▶ Helpful Forms for Your Job Search

If you're engaged in an active job search, it's important to track your activities to be sure you keep information about potential employers well-organized for quick access. Included here is a form to help you track the companies you've applied to and any interview activities that occur. You will also find a form for assessing your performance in your job interviews, and one for evaluating whether each opportunity is appropriate for you. Also included is contributor Tamara Dowling's slightly different approach to an interview self-evaluation.

Job-Search Activities

Company	Resume Sent	First Interview	First Follow-Up	Second Interview	Second Follow-Up	Comments
Mega Industries	6/29/08	7/8/08	7/15/08	7/29/08	8/6/08	Anticipate decision by 9/1/08
Acme Manufacturing	7/1/08	7/16/08	7/21/08	8/1/08	8/3/08	Received Job Offer 8/6/08

Post-Interview Self-Assessment

Company Name: _____

Interviewer: _____

Position: _____   Interview Date: _____

- Arrived on time?

- Had all information needed to complete the application?

- Was friendly to everyone, including the receptionist?

- Maintained eye contact?

- Spoke clearly and with purpose?

- Did not interrupt?

- Supported answers with specific examples of achievements?

- Shook interviewer's hand firmly at beginning and end of interview?

- Asked specific, intelligent questions that were not already answered?

- Conveyed benefits that I could deliver to the company?

- Presented a professional image?

- Obtained interviewer's business card?

- Understand next steps following interview?

- Gave interviewer clean, professional copy of resume?

To further evaluate your performance, ask yourself these questions:

- What did I learn about the company that I did not know before?

- What clues did I get from the interviewer about his/her interest?

- What would I do differently next time?

Tamara Dowling, CPRW

SeekingSuccess.com

Sample Opportunity Evaluation

Item	Priority Rating	Compatibility Rating	Comments
Was the job content as anticipated or otherwise still to your liking?	1	B	
Did you learn new information about expectations such as travel, routine work schedule, or overtime?	1	B	Yes—didn't discuss in detail yet.
Will you have the opportunity to meet your prospective direct supervisor prior to a hiring decision? Did you connect in a positive way with this individual?	1	B	Yes, met briefly. Was told he would interview next round.
Do you feel positive about any colleagues you met?	2	B	Only briefly. Seemed nice.
Did the overall "feel" of the place seem appropriate/comfortable to you?	1	A	
Did the interviewer(s) respond to your questions openly and provide the information you requested?	2	A	
Did you learn new information about the organization's future plans that impact your level of interest in the position?	2	A	Just awarded big, new contract!
Did you learn anything new about the organization's history or status (such as pending lawsuits or recent or imminent policy changes)?	2		No news.
Did you have the opportunity to observe your work area? Was an opportunity to do so discussed?	2	B	
Did you learn anything new about your work location that impacts your level of interest in the position?	2	A	On bus route. Perfect backup for bad weather days.
Did you learn anything about additional training or education that may be required for your target position? How about availability and accessibility of professional development within the organization?	2	A	Great tuition assistance program!
Were the success criteria for the position reasonable in your opinion?	1	B	Great expectations!
Is this a newly created position? If not, did you learn why the incumbent or recent incumbent is leaving/left?	2	C	Sounds like there may have been "issues"—hope to learn more in future discussions.
Did you learn how the target position fits in to the big picture?	2	B	Hope to learn more.
Did you learn about potential future advancement within the organization?	1	B	Hope to learn more.

Sample Interview Self-Evaluation

Company:	Date: Interviewer:	
Item	Notes/Ways I Could Improve in the Future	Rating
Arrived on time? Early?		
Wardrobe appropriate?		
Good solid handshake?		
Good eye contact?		
Went prepared with all necessary info to complete company application if requested?		
Listened and responded clearly and articulately?		
Demonstrated my strong interest in and research on the organization?		
Clarified job expectations and how target position fits into the big picture?		
Shared stories in response to questions that show past successes relevant to prospective employer?		
Overcame interviewer's objections to perceived obstacles to selection?		
Responded to questions with a positive attitude (without criticizing prior employers or shifting accountability)? Which questions were the most challenging (if any)?		
Asked your own questions of the interviewer at appropriate time(s) and requested clarification as appropriate?		
Remembered to capture names and/or business cards from everyone you met?		
Remembered to thank the receptionist or other support personnel?		
Closed with expression of your desire for the position and your thanks to the interviewer(s)?		

Appendix C

▶ Favorite Resources From the Pros

Please note: Many of the following tips include Websites. Because the Internet is constantly evolving, some sites may have relocated or otherwise been changed. As of this writing, all sites were fully functional.

Company Research

From Marilyn A. Feldstein, MPA, JCTC, MBTI, PHR—Career Coach and Professional Speaker:

Beyond visiting the official Website, scanning related journals and other publications, be sure to contact local staffing companies to supplement your research on the target employer and/or hiring manager.

From Harriette Royer, MS—Director of Consulting and Education, Career Management Center, Simon Graduate School of Business, University of Rochester:

MarketLine, formerly Data Monitor, is a resource that is well-researched, clearly written, and contains comprehensive company and industry trend information. In about 20 minutes, candidates can adequately supplement the company Website information and general research using MarketLine's overview of the company's mission, vision, and competitive advantage within the industries in which it competes. MarketLine should be available to most through their public library or regional college library.

Savvy candidates use its SWOT analysis, which articulates the company's strengths, weaknesses, opportunities, and threats in light of the competition and industry trends, to identify areas where they can make a contribution. They will identify at least a couple of ways in which their skills and experience could contribute to the company building on its strengths, overcoming a weakness, exploiting an opportunity or confronting a threat. The SWOT analysis also provides an excellent stimulus for candidates' questions about the company and for building the case about their assets for the position.

From Joanne Fasolo Shugrue, CPRW, GCDF—Hartford CT Works, Connecticut Department of Labor:

Two great Websites that can help you gather relevant occupational data for your interview, survey current industry compensation standards, and even assist you in preparing your resume and cover letter are: *www.online.onetcenter.org* and *www.careerinfonet.org/acinet/EmployabilityCheckup*. *www.online.onetcenter.org* contains information on specific careers, including:

▶ Tasks and work activities.

▶ Required tools and technology.

▶ Necessary skills and abilities.

▶ Educational requirements.

▶ Work styles and work values.

▶ Wages and employment trends (select a state—it reveals statewide average salary ranges, both annual and hourly).

The site *www.careerinfonet.org/acinet/EmployabilityCheckup* contains information including the following:

▶ Employment criteria.

▶ Occupational employment trends by city from 2004 through 2014.

▶ Industry employment trends.

▶ Local and state unemployment rates.

▶ Educational/training attainment by occupation.

▶ Wages by city.

▶ Pluses, minuses, and average occupational outlooks.

From Makini Theresa Harvey, CPRW, JCTC, CEIP, CCM—Career Abundance:

Don't overlook social networking sites, such as www.LinkedIn.com, to learn more about companies and hiring managers. Also, many companies have begun searching the social networking profiles to find their ideal candidates. Other sites to check out for company research include:

▶ Hoover's Inc.: *www.hoovers.com*

▶ Company Sleuth: *www.companysleuth.com*

▶ Business Wire: *www.businesswire.com*

▶ The Security and Exchange Commission: *www.sec.gov*

▶ CEO Express: *www.ceoexpress.com*

▶ Wikipedia: *www.wikipedia.com* (once you're at the site, type in the company name)

Researching Industry Trends

Weddles Journals: *www.weddles.com*

Department of Labor, Bureau of Labor and Statistics: *www.bls.gov*

Society of Human Resource Management: *www.shrm.org*

Another excellent job search resource is *www.job-hunt.org*. This Website is full of outstanding articles, job search tips, industry trends, career resources, and more, whether you are just getting into the hunt or a corporate warrior.

Researching Nonprofit Employers

From Gail Smith Boldt, Arnold-Smith Associates:

Most nonprofit entities are required to make available for public inspection their annual tax returns, including IRS "Form 990," Return of Organization Exempt From Income Tax. Information displayed on these forms may give you a sense of the financial viability of the organization. These Websites also contain other key information on many nonprofits:

www.FoundationCenter.org

www.guidestar.org

www.erieri.com (Economic Research Institute)

Researching Salary Information

From Louise Garver, CPRW, MCDP, CMP, JCTC, CLBF, CPBS, CEIP, COIS— Career Directions LLC:

The Internet is a great resource for free and fee-based data on the salary ranges for different positions in various industries—geographically. These sites include *www.salary.com* (user-friendly compilation of data from other sources), *www.careerjournal.com* (click on Salaries by Industry) for links to salary tables and articles, and *www.jobstar.org* (provides access to a few hundred online salary surveys). Another site that offers salary reports and cost of living data is *www.paq.com* (PAQ's Salary Report). A fee-based site, *www.payscale.com*, will provide customized salary information for positions that are more difficult to find on the fee sites. Robert Half International publishes regional Salary Guides for different occupations such as accounting, banking, financial services and technology—all at no charge. Just visit *www.roberthalf.com* to print a copy online.

Recommended Books

Competency-Based Interviews: Master the Tough New Interview Style and Give Them the Answers That Will Win You the Job by Robin Kessler (Career Press).

Job Search Bloopers: Every Mistake You Can Make on the Road to Career Suicide...And How to Avoid Them by Laura DeCarlo and Susan Guarnari (Career Press).

Knock 'em Dead: The Ultimate Job Search Guide by Martin Yate, CPC (Adams Media).

Negotiating Your Salary: How to Make $1,000 a Minute by Jack Chapman (Ten Speed Press).

No-Nonsense Cover Letters: The Essential Guide to Creating Attention-Grabbing Cover Letters That Get Interviews & Job Offers by Arnold Boldt and Wendy Enelow (Career Press).

No-Nonsense Resumes: The Essential Guide to Creating Attention-Grabbing Resumes That Get Interviews & Job Offers by Arnold Boldt and Wendy Enelow (Career Press).

Resumes for the Rest of Us: Secrets from the Pros for Job Seekers with Unconventional Career Paths by Arnold Boldt (Career Press).

Secrets of Power Salary Negotiating: Inside Secrets from a Master Negotiator by Roger Dawson (Career Press).

10 Insider Secrets to a Winning Job Search: Everything You Need to Get the Job You Want in 24 Hours—Or Less by Todd Bermont (Career Press).

Appendix D

▶ List of Contributors

The following professional career coaches and resume writers have contributed their tips on how to do your best in job interviews, which appear throughout *No-Nonsense Job Interviews*. All have years of experience helping job seekers attain their goals; many have earned distinguishing professional credentials, including:

CARW	Certified Advanced Resume Writer
CCM	Credentialed Career Master
CCMC	Certified Career Management Coach
CCRE	Certified Career Research Expert
CCTJ	Certified Career Transition Jumpmaster
CDFT	Career Development Facilitator Training
CECC	Certified Electronic Career Coach
CEIP	Certified Employment Interview Professional
CERW	Certified Expert Resume Writer
CFRW / CC	Certified Federal Resume Writer/Career Coach
CHRP	Certified Human Resources Professional
CIS	Certified Interview Strategist
CLBF	Certified Life Blueprint Facilitator
CMP	Certified Management Professional
CPBS	Certified Personal Brand Strategist
CPC	Certified Personnel Consultant

CRW	Certified Resume Writer
CPRW	Certified Professional Resume Writer
CRS	Certified Resume Strategist
CTMS	Certified Transition Management Seminars
CTP	Career Transition Professional
CTSB	Certified Targeted Small Business
CWDP	Certified Workforce Development Professional
FIRO-B	Fundamental Interpersonal Relations Orientation-Behavior Assessments
FRWCC	Federal Resume Writer & Career Coach
GCDF	Global Career Development Facilitator
IJCTC	International Job and Career Transition Coach
JCTC	Job and Career Transition Coach
MBTI	(Certified in) Myers-Briggs Temperament Instrument
MCC	Master Career Counselor
MCDP	Master Career Development Professional
MCD	Master Career Director
NCC	Nationally Certified Counselor
NCCC	Nationally Certified Career Coach
NCRW	Nationally Certified Resume Writer
PHR	Professional in Human Resources
RPR	Registered Professional Recruiter
VAL	Values Arrangement List Administrator

Doris Appelbaum, President
Appelbaum's Resume Prof., Inc.
Milwaukee, WI
dorisa@execpc.com
www.appelbaumresumes.com
800-619-9777 / 414-352-5994

Deanne Arnath, CPRW
A Résumé Wizard & Services
Arlington, TX
deanne@aresumewizard.com
www.aresumewizard.com
866-422-0800

Laurie Berenson, CPRW
Sterling Career Concepts, LLC
Park Ridge, NJ
laurie@sterlingcareerconcepts.com
www.sterlingcareerconcepts.com
201-573-8282

Gail Smith Boldt
Arnold-Smith Associates
Gail@ResumeSOS.com
www.ResumeSOS.com
585-383-0350

Heather Carson, CPRW, GCDF, JCTC, CWDP
Second Start
Rochester, NH
hcarson@second-start.org
www.second-start.org
603-344-8076

Clay Cerny, PhD
AAA Targeted Writing & Coaching Services
Chicago, IL
info@aaatargeted.com
www.aaatargeted.com
773-907-8660

Freddie Cheek, MS Ed, CCM, CPRW, CARW, CWDP
Cheek & Associates
Amherst, NY
fscheek@cheekandassociates.com
www.CheekandAssociates.com
716-835-6945

Norine Dagliano, NCRW, CPRW, CFRW/CC
ekm Inspirations
Hagerstown, MD
norine@ekminspirations.com
www.ekminspirations.com
301-766-2032

Pierre G. Daunic, PhD, CCM, CRW, CECC
Fast Forward Career Services, LLC
Westerville, OH
Pierre@fastforwardcareers.com
www.fastforwardcareers.com
614-895-9989

Laura DeCarlo, BA, CERW, CCM, CEIC, JCTC, CECC, CWDP
Executive Director
Career Directors International
laura@careerdirectors.com
Tamara Dowling, CPRW
SeekingSuccess.com
Valencia, CA
td@seekingsuccess.com
www.seekingsuccess.com
661-903-0696

Robyn L. Feldberg, CCMC, NCRW, VAL
Abundant Success Career Services
Frisco, TX
Robyn@AbundantSuccessCareerServices.com
www.AbundantSuccessCareerServices.com
866-WIN-AJOB (946-2562)

Marilyn A. Feldstein, MPA, JCTC, MBTI, PHR
Career Choices Unlimited, Inc.
Jacksonville, FL
mfeldstein@bellsouth.net
www.careerchoicesunlimited.com
904-262-9470 / 904-443-0059

Cliff Flamer, CPRW, NCRW, NCC
BrightSide Résumés
Oakland, CA
writers@brightsideresumes.com
www.brightsideresumes.com
877-668-9767 / 510-444-1724

Gail Frank, NCRW, CPRW, JCTC, CEIP
Employment U
Tampa, FL
gailfrank@post.harvard.edu
www.EmploymentU.com
813-926-1353

Louise Garver, JCTC, CPRW, CLBF, CEIP, CMP, CPBS
Career Directions, LLC
Hartford, CT
LouiseGarver@cox.net
www.CareerDirectionsLLC.com
860-623-9476

Makini Theresa Harvey, CPRW, JCTC, CEIP, CCM
Career Abundance
Menlo Park, CA
makini@careerabundance.com
www.careerabundance.com
650-630-7610

Connie Hauer, CEIP
CareerPro Services
Sartell, MN
chauer@mncareerpro.com
www.mncareerpro.com
320-260-6569

Loretta Heck
All Word Services
Prospect Heights, IL
siegfried@ameritech.net
www.allwordservices.com
847-215-7517

Diane Irwin
Dynamic Résumés
Cherry Hill, NJ
dynamicresumes@comcast.net
www.dynamicresumesofNJ.com
856-321-0092

Susan P. Joyce, MBA
NETability, Inc.
Marlborough, MA
sjoyce@netability.com
www.Job-Hunt.org
508-624-6261

Brian Leeson, M Sc
Vector Consultants Pty Ltd
Echunga, South Australia
Australia
brian@vectorconsultants.com.au
+61 8 8388 8183

Murray A. Mann, CCM, CPBS
Global Diversity Solutions Group
Chicago, IL
Murray@GlobalDiversitySolutions.com
www.GlobalDiversitySolutions.com
312-404-3108

Melanie Noonan
Peripheral Pro, LLC
West Paterson, NJ
PeriPro1@aol.com
973-785-3011

Kris Plantrich, CPRW, CEIP
RésuméWonders
Ortonville, MI
support@resumewonders.com
www.resumewonders.com
248-627-2624
888-789-2081

Dawn L. Rasmussen, CTP, CMP
Pathfinder Writing and Career Services, LLC
Portland, OR
dawn@pathfindercareers.com
www.pathfindercareers.com
503-539-3954

Harriette Royer, MS
Director of Consulting & Education
Career Management Center
Simon Graduate School of Business
University of Rochester
Rochester, NY
Harriette.Royer@simon.rochester.edu
585-275-0137

Camille Carboneau Roberts, CFRW/C,
CPRW, CEIP, CARW, CCRE
CC Computer Services & Training
Idaho Falls, ID
Camille@SuperiorResumes.com
www.SuperiorResumes.com
208-522-4455

Barbara Safani, CPRW, NCRW, CERW,
CCM
Career Solvers
New York, NY
info@careersolvers.com
www.careersolvers.com
866-333-1800

Joanne Fasolo Shugrue, CPRW, GCDF
Hartford CT Works
Connecticut Dept. of Labor
Hartford, CT
joanne.shugrue@ct.gov
www.ctdol.state.ct.us
860-256-3688

Tanya Taylor, CRS, CHRP
TNT Human Resources Management
Toronto, Ontario
Canada
info@tntresumewriter.com
www.tntresumewriter.com
416-887-5819

Rose Mary Bombela-Tobias
Global Diversity Solutions Group
Chicago, IL
GlobalDiversitySolutions.com
312-404-3108

Edward Turilli, MA, CPRW
AccuWriter Resume Service
North Kingstown, RI
edtur@cox.net
Resumes4-u.com
401-268-3020

Pearl White, CPRW, JCTC, CEIP
A 1st Impression Résumé Service
Irvine, CA
pearlwhite1@cox.net
www.a1stimpression.com
949-651-1068

Daisy Wright, CCM, CDP
The Wright Career Solution
Brampton, Ontario
Canada
careercoach@thewrightcareer.com
www.thewrightcareer.com
www.nocanadianexperience-eh.com
905-840-7039

*I*ndex

About the Author

Arnie Boldt has been helping job seekers since 1994, when he founded Arnold-Smith Associates along with his wife, Gail Smith Boldt. The firm has assisted thousands of job seekers in transition, including coaching them on interviewing strategies and techniques. He and Gail have conducted workshops on interviewing, and consulted one-on-one with candidates to help them refine and practice their job interviewing skills.

Known as one of the country's leading resume writers, Arnie is the coauthor of *No-Nonsense Resumes* and *No-Nonsense Cover Letters*, and the author of *Resumes for the Rest of Us* (all published by Career Press), and has contributed to nearly 40 books on resume writing and job-search topics.

He is a five-time TORI (Toast of the Resume Industry) Awards nominee in the categories of best creative resume (twice), best cover letter (twice), and best return-to-work resume. He has spoken on job search–related topics to groups in the healthcare and manufacturing fields, and has delivered presentations developed especially for older workers and executives in transition. In addition, he's been quoted in articles appearing on CareerJournal.com and FoxBusiness.com, and has been a guest on local television and radio programs in Rochester, New York.

Arnie holds a bachelor's degree in technical communications from Clarkson University and is a certified professional resume writer, and a job and career transition coach. His versatility and multifaceted professional background combine to give him the expertise required to successfully work with the broadest array of clients from a wide range of career fields. He prides himself on his experience assisting clients ranging from tradespeople to new graduates to seasoned corporate executives, and everyone in between. A lifelong resident of Upstate New York, he and Gail share a home with their two Chihuahuas in a suburb of Rochester.